GROSSET'S

JUST POINT!

A PICTURE DICTIONARY FOR TRAVELERS

BY HERSCHEL LEVIT
& EDITH HARRIS GUGGENHEIM

Illustrations by Herschel Levit

GROSSET & DUNLAP, INC.
A National General Company

Publishers New York

Library of Congress Catalog Card No.: 72-183022
ISBN: 0-448-00654-5

Published Simultaneously in Canada

Printed in the United States of America

CONTENTS

At the Hotel 2
Im Hotel 2
En el Hotel 2
A l'Hôtel 2
In Albergo 2

Changing Money 6
Geldwechsel 6
Cambio 6
Change 6
Cambio 6

At the Restaurant 8
Meats, 10; Fish, 14; Eggs, 16; Vegtables, 18; Potatoes, 22; Pasta, 23; Bread, 24; Cheese, 25; Fruit, 26; Dessert, 28; Coffee/Tea, 30; Soup/Salad, 31; Drinks, 32

Im Restaurant 8
Fleisch, 10; Fisch, 14; Eier, 16; Gemüse, 18; Kartoffeln, 22; Pasta, 23; Brot, 24; Kase, 25; Frucht, 26; Nachtisch, 28; Kaffee/Tee, 30; Suppe/Salat, 31; Getränke, 32

En el Restaurante 8
Carne, 10; Pescado, 14; Huevos, 16; Legumbres, 18; Papas, 22; Pasta, 23; Pan, 24; Queso, 25; Fruta, 26; Postres, 28; Café/Té, 30; Sopa/Ensalada, 31; Bebidas, 32

Au Restaurant 8
Viande, 10; Poisson, 14; Oeufs, 16; Légumes, 18; Pommes de Terre, 22; Pâte, 23; Pain, 24; Fromage, 25; Fruit, 26; Déssert, 28; Café/Té, 30; Soupe/Salade, 31; Boissons, 32

Nel Ristorante 8
Carne, 10; Pesce, 14; Uova, 16; Legumi, 18; Patate, 22; Pasta, 23; Pane, 24; Formaggio, 25; Frutta, 26; Dolci, 28; Caffè/Tè, 30; Zuppa/Insalata, 31; Bibite, 32

Dates and Time 34
Daten und Zeiten 34
Datas y Tiempos 34
Dates et Temps 34
Date e Tempi 34

Beauty Parlor 38
Schönheitssalon 38
Salón de Belleza 38
Salon de Beauté 38
Salone di Bellezza 38

Barber Shop 40
Barbier Salon 40
Salón de Barbero 40
Salon de Barbier 40
Salone di Barbiere 40

Mail 42
Post 42
Corréo 42
Courrier 42
Posta 42

Stationery 46
Schreibwaren 46
Papel 46
Papeterie 46
Cartiera 46

Baggage 50
Gepäck 50
Equipaje 50
Bagages 50
Bagaglio 50

Getting Around by Plane 54
Flugzeugreisen 54
Viajando por Avión 54
Voyage par Avion 54
Viaggi coll'Aereo 54

Getting Around by Train 56
Zugfahrten 56
Viajando por Tren 56
Voyage par le Train 56
Viaggi per Treno 56

Getting Around by Ship 60
Schiffahrten 60
Viajando por Buque 60
Voyage en Bateau 60
Viaggi per Nave 60

Getting Around by Car 66
Autofahrten 66
Viajando por Autómovil 66
Voyage en Voiture 66
Viaggi in Macchina 66

Shopping 86
Drugstore, 86; Tobacco, 92; Sewing, 94; Clothing, 96; Gifts, 110; Camera, 120
Einkaufe Machen 86
Apotheke, 86; Tabak, 92; Nähen, 94; Kleider, 96; Geschenke, 110; Kamera, 120
Hacer Compras 86
Farmacia, 86; Tabaco, 92; Coser, 94; Vestidos, 96; Regalos, 110; Camera, 120
Faire des Achats 86
Pharmacie, 86; Tabac, 92; Coudre, 94; Vêtements, 96; Cadeaux, 110; Appareil Photographique, 120
Fare delle Compare 86
Farmacia, 86; Tabacco, 92; Cucire, 94; Vestiti, 96; Regali, 110; Macchina Fotografica, 120

Sightseeing 124
Besuchen von Sehenswürdigkeiten 124
Visita de Puntos de Interés 124
Tourisme 124
Girare per Vedere le Curiosità 124

Amusements 128
Unterhaltungen 128
Diversiones 128
Divertissements 128
Divertimenti 128

Games 132
Spiele 132
Juegos 132
Jeux 132
Giochi 132

Sports 135
Sport 135
Deportes 135
Sport 135

Camping 150
Camping 150
Camping 150
Camping 150
Campeggio 150

Emergencies 152
Notfälle 152
Emergencias 152
Urgences 152
Emergenze 152

Health 158
Gesundheit 158
Salud 158
Sante 158
Salute 158

A Word about This Book

Sooner or later even the most sophisticated and linguistically talented traveler will find himself in a land where he has small or no command of the native tongue. Perhaps in Kenya or Burma, perhaps in a neighboring land. No matter, here is a book that solves many problems. *Just Point!* is what is needed when you do not speak the native language. It contains hundreds of detailed drawings of specific items that you, the traveler, may want or need. It shows the situations you are most likely to encounter—from dining to shelter to transportation to clothing and gifts and entertainment. With this book in hand you do not need to search a dictionary for a word that may, in any case, not be included in an abridged vocabulary. Once you have found the picture in this book, all you have to do is point to it. To aid you in finding the needed illustration, complete indexes in five major languages are included in the back of the book. In addition, here are two basic phrases, in these languages, that can be used with the pictures. They have been broadly transliterated as well, using symbols of the International Phonetic Alphabet. If, however, you cannot manage these pronunciations, still all you have to do to use the phrases is *just point* at them.

I would like... (ai wud laik)	*Where is...* (hwer iz)
Ich möchte... (iç møç-tə)	*Wo ist...* (vo ist)
Quisiera... (ki-sye-ra)	*Dónde está...* (don-dɛ ɛs-ta)
Je voudrais... (ʒə vu-drɛ)	*Où est...* (u ɛ)
Vorrei... (vor-rɛi)	*Dov'è...* (do-vɛ)

Über Dieses Buch

Es kann leicht vorkommen das sogar der geübteste und sprächlich talentierteste Reisende sich in einem Land findet wo er wenig oder keinen Begriff der einheimischen Sprache hat; vielleicht in Kenya oder Burma, vielleicht in einem gränzenden Land. Das macht aber nichts, weil hier ist ein Buch das viele Probleme löst. *Nur Zeigen* ist die Antwort wenn Sie nicht die einheimische Sprache kennen. Est enthält Hunderte detailierte Zeichnungen der Dinge die Sie wunschen oder benötigen. Es zeigt Ihnen die Situationen welche Sie öfters begegnem werden—Mahalzeiten, Unterkunft, Transportation, Kleidung, Geschenke, oder Unterhaltungen. Mit diesem Buch in der Hand brauchen Sie in keinem Diktionär suchen um ein Wort zu finden das, vielleicht sogar in einem abgekürztem Wörterbuch nicht zu finden ist. Sobald Sie das richtige Bild gefunden haben, brauchen Sie es nur zu zeigen. Um Ihnen zu helfen das nötige Bild zu finden, behält das Buch komplette Register in fünf Sprachen. Ausserdem gehen mit jeder Zeichnung zwei basische Phrasen in diesen fünf Sprachen. Diese Phrasen sind phonetisch gedruckt in den Symbolen des Internationalen Phonetischen Alphabet. Aber sogar wenn sie diese Phrasen nicht aussprechen können, haben Sie doch *nur* auf sie zu *Zeigen*.

Ich möchte. . . (iç møç-tə) *Wo ist*. . . (vo ist)
Quisiera. . . (ki-sye-ra) *Dónde está*. . . (don-dɛ ɛs-ta)
Je voudrais. . . (ʒə vu-drɛ) *Où est*. . . (u ɛ)
Vorrei. . . (vor-rɛi) *Dov'è*. . . (do-vɛ)
I would like. . . (ai wud laik) *Where is*. . . (hwer iz)

Unas Palabras Acerca de Este Libro.

Tarde o temprano aún el viajante más sofisticado y linguísticamente talentoso se encontrará en tierra donde tiene muy poco o ningún conocimiento de la lengua nativa. Quizás en Kenya o Burma. Quizás en un país vecino. No importa, aquí tiene un libro que resuelve muchos problemas JUST POINT! es lo que usted necesita cuando no habla la lengua nativa. Este libro contiene centenas de dibujos detallados acerca de artículos específicos que usted el viajante vaya a necesitar o desee saber. Ilustra las situaciones en cuales usted probablemente se encontrará—desde comida, alojamiento, o transportación, a ropa, regalos, entretenimiento. Con este libro en mano usted no necesitará de diccionarios que probablemente ni siquiera contengan las palabras deseadas. Una vez que usted encuentre el dibujo correcto, lo unico que tiene que hacer es enseñarlo. Haciéndolo más facil para usted, hemos copilado en la parte de atrás del libro indices completos en los cinco idiomas principales. En adición hay dos frases básicas en estos idiomas que puede usted usar con los dibujos. Estas frases han sido también interpretadas en los símbolos del alfabeto fonético internacional. Sin embargo, si usted no logra la pronunciatión correcta, todo lo que necesita hacer para usarlas es SEÑALAR.

Quisiera. . . (ki-sye-ra) *Dónde está. . .* (don-dɛ ɛs-ta)
Je voudrais. . . (ʒə vu-drɛ) *Où est. . .* (u ɛ)
Vorrei. . . (vor-rɛi) *Dov'è. . .* (do-vɛ)
I would like. . . (ai wud laik) *Where is. . .* (hwer iz)
Ich möchte. . . (iç møç-tə) *Wo ist. . .* (vo ist)

Sur ce Livre

Le voyageur intelligent même sachant des langues etrangères tôt ou tard se trouvera dans un lieu où il ne saura pas parler la langue du pays. Ce sera peut-être au Kenia ou en Birmanie, ou peut-être un pays voisin. N'importe. Voici un livre qui peut résoudre beaucoup de problèmes. *Just Point* est un livre utile lorsqu'on ne parle pas la langue du pays où on se trouve. Ce livre contient des centaines de desseins detaillés des choses dont a besoin le voyageur, des articles qu'il désire. *Just Point* traîte des sujets suivants—le manger, le logement, le transport, les vêtements, les achats, les divertissements. Ce livre en main, vous n'êtes pas obligé de chercher dans le dictionnaire un mot qui, la plupart du temps, dans une édition réduite ne se trouve même pas. Une fois que vous trouvez dans ce livre l'image de ce que vous désirez vous n'avez qu'à la montrer à quelqu'un. Pour vous aider à trouver le dessein dont vous avez besoin, il y a des indexes alphabétiques en cinq langues principales. En outre, il y a deux phrases essentielles dans chaque langue, dont vous pouvez vous servir avec les desseins. Ces phrases ont été transcrités en l'alphabet de l'Association Phonétique Internationale. Cependent, si vous ne connaissez pas cette prononciation, vous n'avez qu'à montrer du doigt la phrase en question.

Je voudrais... (ʒə vu-drɛ)
Vorrei... (vor-rɛi)
I would like... (ai wud laik)
Ich möchte... (iç møç-tə)
Quisiera... (ki-sye-ra)

Où est... (u ɛ)
Dov'è... (do-vɛ)
Where is... (hwer iz)
Wo ist... (vo ist)
Dónde está... (don-dɛ ɛs-ta)

Due Parole su Questo Libro

Presto o tardi, anche il viaggiatore più preparato e con predisposizione alle lingue viene a trovarsi in un paese dove ha una scarsa o nulla padronanza della lingua locale: forse in Kenia o a Burma, forse in un paese vicino. Non importa, ecco un libro che risolve molti problemi. *Just Point!* è quello che occorre quando non parlate la lingua del luogo. Contiene centinaia di particolareggiate illustrazioni di specifici oggetti di cui Voi viaggiatore potreste avere voglia o bisogno. Mostra le situazioni in cui molto probabilmente verrebbe a trovarvi, dal cibo all'alloggio, al trasporto, all'abbiliamento, ai regali e ai divertimenti. Con questo libro in mano, non avete bisogno di cercare su un dizionario una parola che in ogni caso potrebbe anche non essere riportata in un vocabulario ridotto. Una volta che avrete trovato l'illustrazione in questo libro, tutto quello che dovrete fare è di indicarla. Per aiutarvi a trovare l'illustrazione che cercate, in fondo al libro si trovano degli indici completi in cinque maggiori lingue. In oltre, vi sono due frasi fondamentali in queste lingue, chi possono essere usate con le illustrazioni. Sono state anche ampiamente trascritte usando i segni dell'alfabeto fonetico internzionale. Si, però, non riuscite a pronunciarle, tutto quello che dovete fare per usarle è di indicarle.

Vorrei. . . (vor-rɛi)
I would like. . . (ai wud laik)
Ich möchte. . . (iç møç-tə)
Quisiera. . . (ki-sye-ra)
Je voudrais. . . (ʒə vu-drɛ)

Dov'è. . . (do-vɛ:)
Where is. . . (hwer iz)
Wo ist. . . (vo ist)
Dónde está. . . (don-dɛ ɛs-ta)
Où est. . . (u ɛ)

Due Parole su Questo Libro

Presto o tardi, anche il viaggiatore più preparato e con predisposizione alle lingue viene a trovarsi in un paese dove ha una scarsa o nulla padronanza della lingua locale: forse in Kenya o a Burma, forse in un paese vicino. Non importa, ecco un libro che risolve molti problemi. *Just Point it* è quello che occorre quando non parlate la lingua del luogo. Contiene centinaia di particolareggiate illustrazioni di specifici oggetti di cui voi viaggiatore potreste avere voglia o bisogno. Illustra le situazioni in cui molto probabilmente verreste a trovarvi, dal cibo all'alloggio, al trasporto, all'abbigliamento, ai regali e ai divertimenti. Con questo libro in mano, non avete bisogno di cercare su un dizionario una parola che in ogni caso potrebbe anche non essere riportata in un vocabolario ridotto. Una volta che avrete trovato l'illustrazione in questo libro, tutto quello che dovete fare è di indicarla. Per aiutarvi a trovare l'illustrazione che cercate in fondo al libro si trovano degli indici completi in alcune maggiori lingue. In oltre, vi sono due frasi fondamentali in queste lingue, che possono essere usate con le illustrazioni. Sono state anche ampiamente trascritte usando i segni dell'alfabeto fonetico internazionale. Se però non riuscite a pronunciarle, tutto quello che dovete fare per usarle è di indicarle.

Vorrei... (vor-rɛi)	*Dov'è...* (do-vɛ)
I would like... (ai wud laik)	*Where is...* (hwer iz)
Ich möchte... (iç mœç-tə)	*Wo ist...* (vo ist)
Quisiera... (ki-sye-ra)	*¿Dónde está...?* (don-de es-ta)
Je voudrais... (ʒə vu-drɛ)	*Où est...* (u ɛ)

GROSSET'S

JUST POINT!

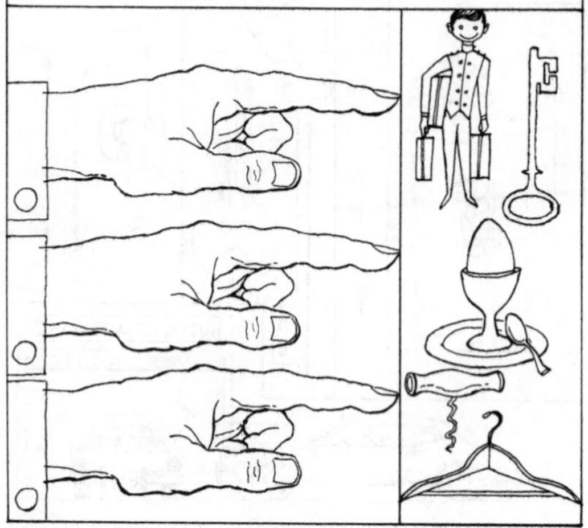

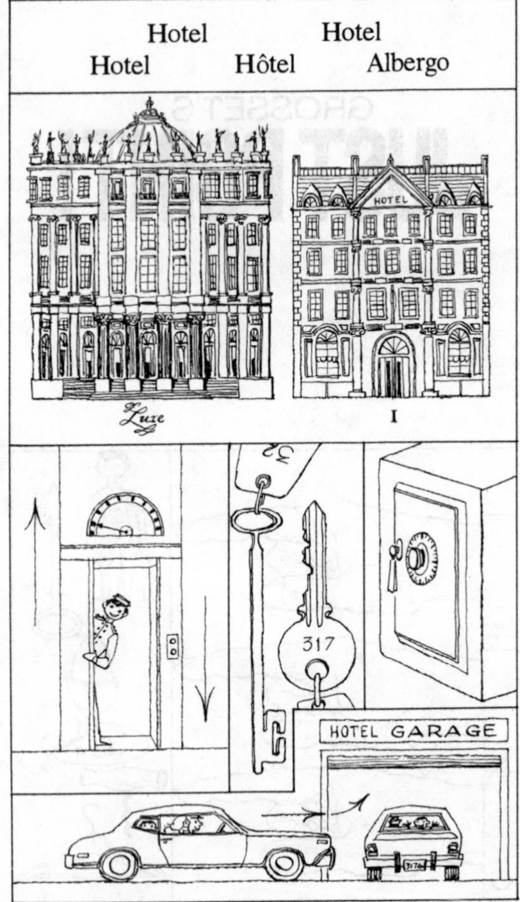
Hotel
Hotel
Hotel
Hôtel
Albergo
HOTEL
Luxe
I
317
HOTEL GARAGE

Hotel Hotel
Hotel Hôtel Albergo
II
III
IV

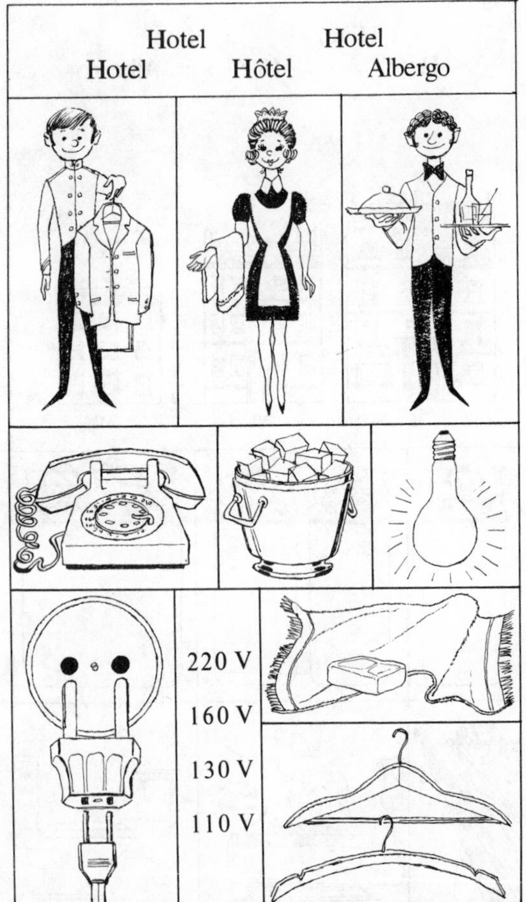
Hotel
Hotel
Hotel
Hôtel
Albergo
220 V
160 V
130 V
110 V

Hotel Hotel
Hotel Hôtel Albergo

Currency Geld
Dinero Cours Denaro
20
FIRST INTERNATIONAL
BANK OF ALL
20
20
20

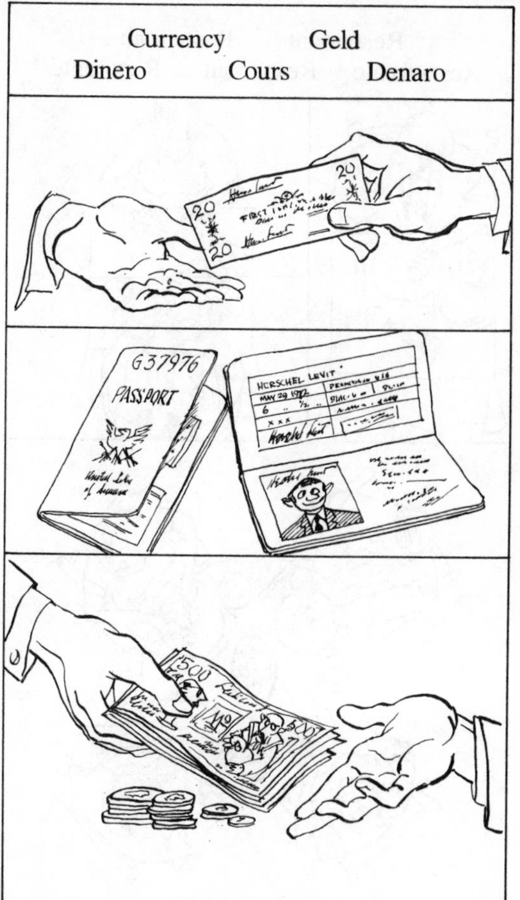
Currency
Geld
Dinero
Cours
Denaro
20
20
20
G37976
PASSPORT
HERSCHEL LEVIT
500

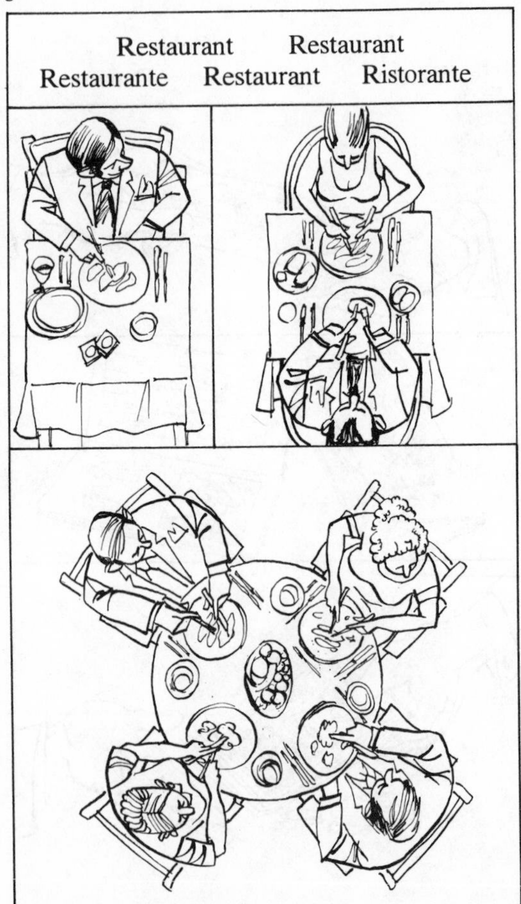
Restaurant Restaurant
Restaurante Restaurant Ristorante

Restaurant Restaurant
Restaurante Restaurant Ristorante
menu

Meats Fleisch
Carne Viande Carne

Meats Fleisch
Carne Viande Carne

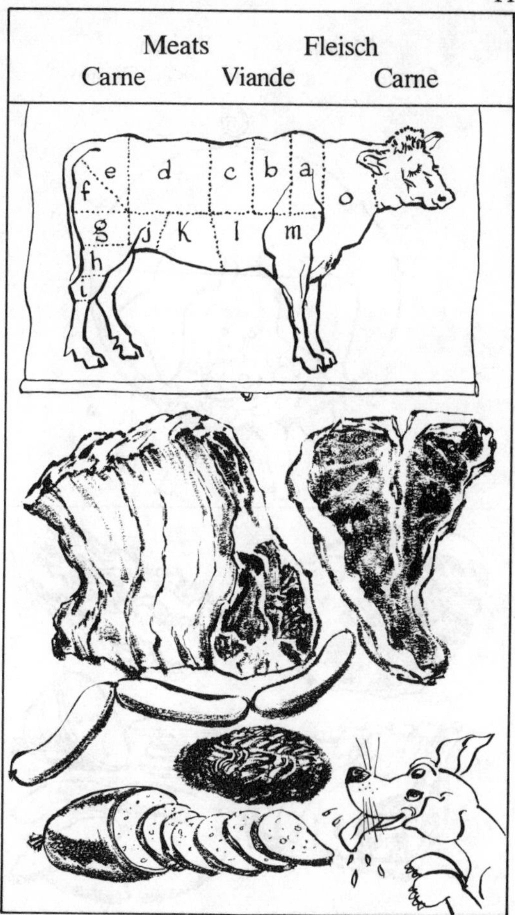

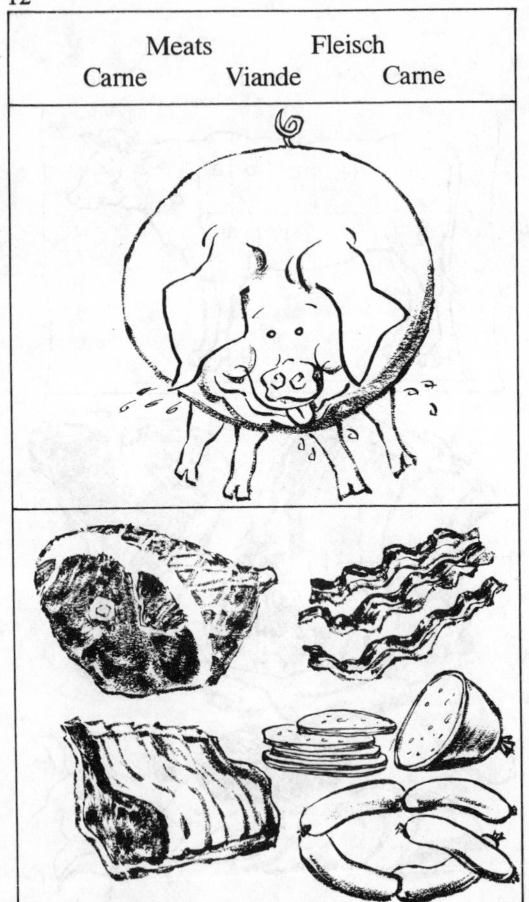
Meats
Fleisch
Carne
Viande
Carne

Meats
Fleisch
Carne
Viande
Carne

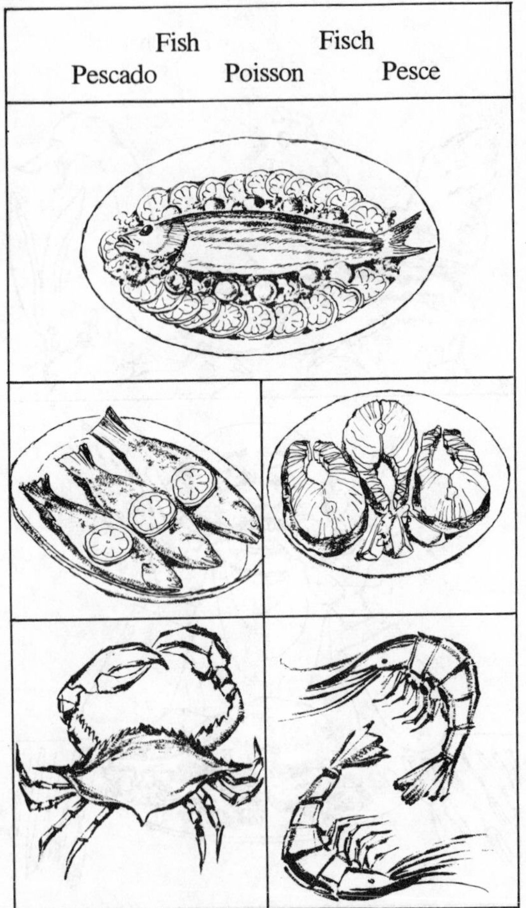
Fish
Fisch
Pescado
Poisson
Pesce

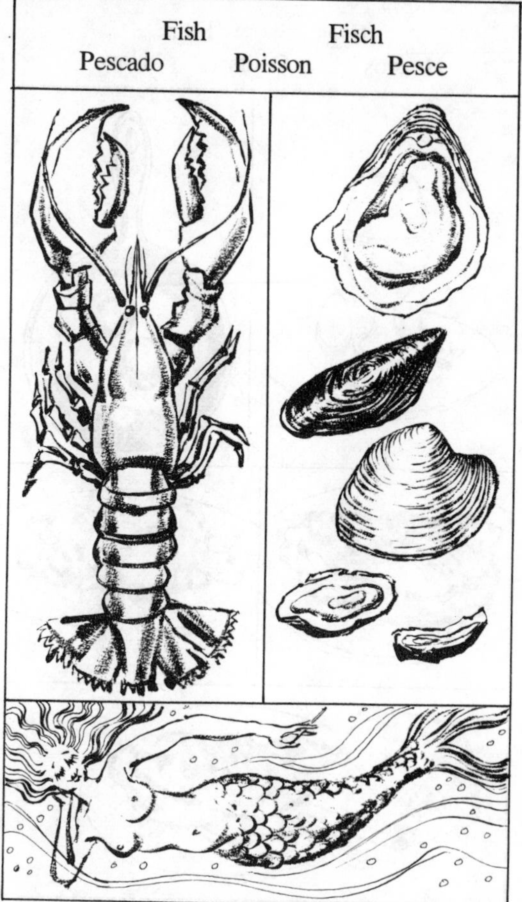

Fish
Fisch
Pescado
Poisson
Pesce

Eggs
Eier
Huevos
Oeufs
Uova

Eggs
Eier
Huevos
Oeufs
Uova

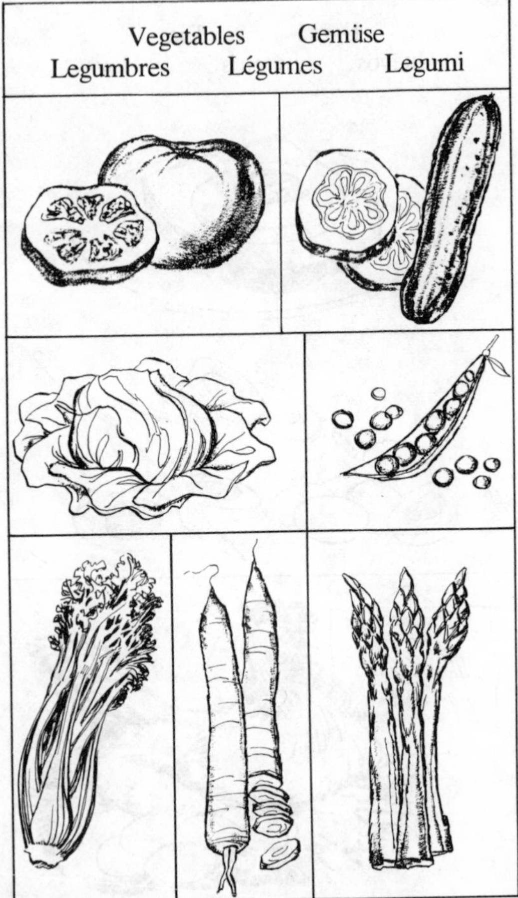
Vegetables Gemüse
Legumbres Légumes Legumi

Vegetables Gemüse
Legumbres Légumes Legumi

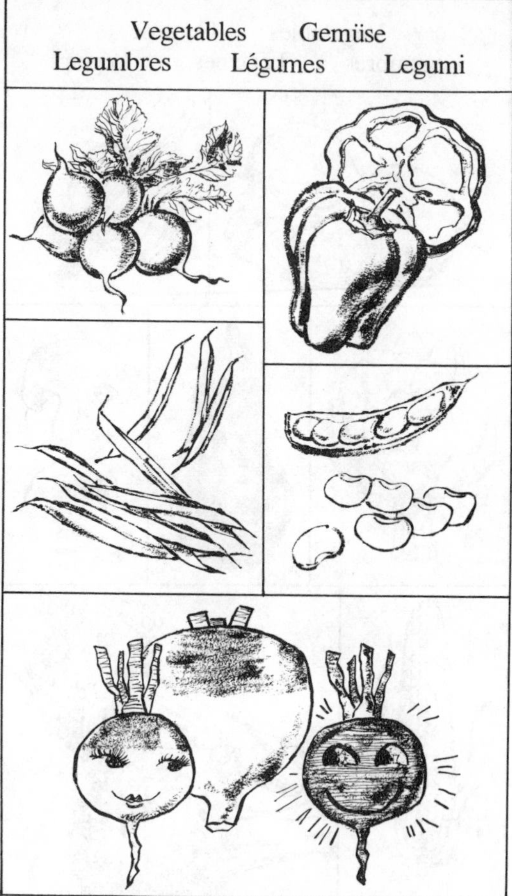

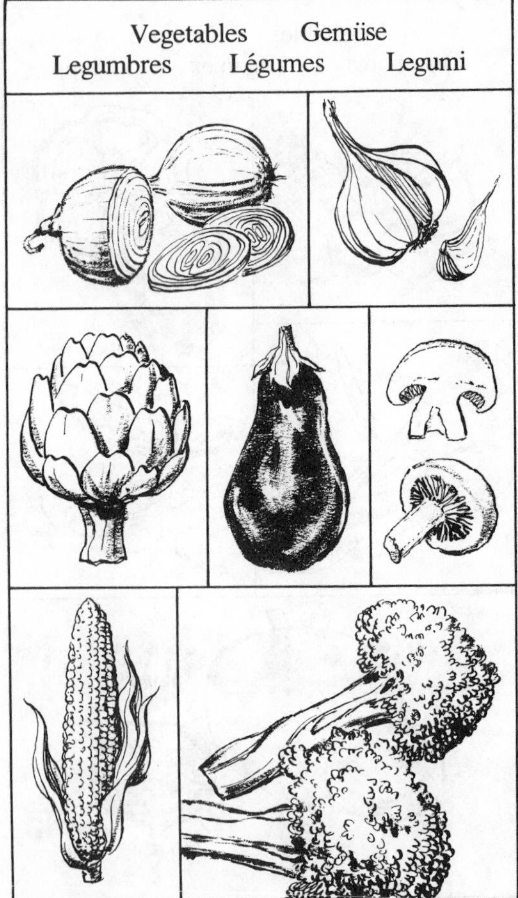
Vegetables Gemüse
Legumbres Légumes Legumi

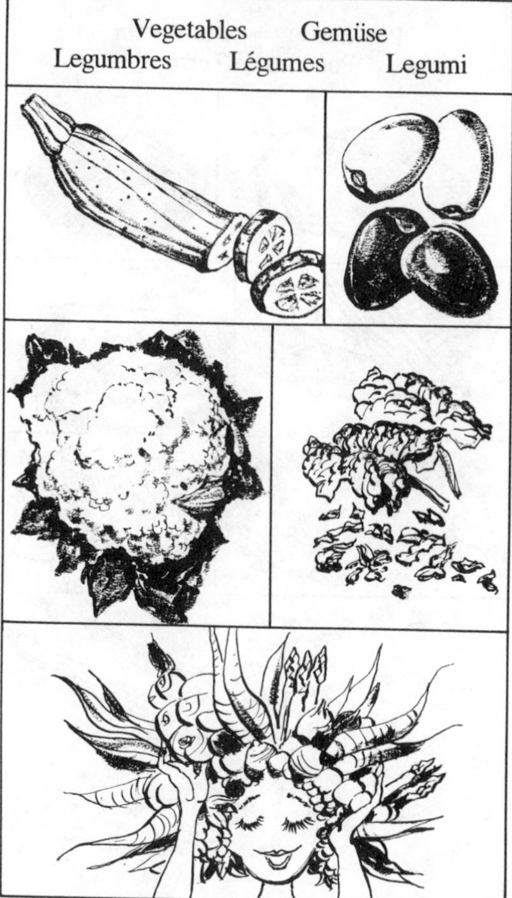
Vegetables Gemüse
Legumbres Légumes Legumi

Potatoes Kartoffeln
Papas Pommes de Terre Patate

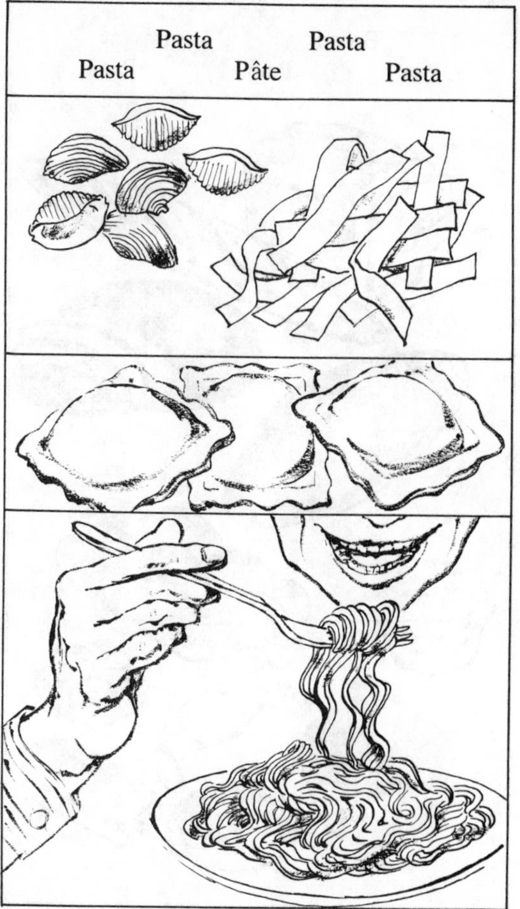
Pasta
Pasta
Pâte
Pasta
Pasta

Bread
Brot
Pan
Pain
Pane

Cheese Käse
Queso Fromage Formaggio

Fruit
Frucht
Fruta
Fruit
Frutta

Fruit Frucht
Fruta Fruit Frutta

Dessert Nachtisch
Postres Déssert Dolci

Dessert Nachtisch

Postres Déssert Dolci

Coffee/Tea Kaffee/Tee
Café/Té Café/Thé Caffè/Tè

Soup/Salad Suppe/Salat
Sopa/Ensalada Soupe/Salade Zuppa/Insalata

Drinks
Getränke
Bebidas
Boissons
Bibite
1961
champagne

Drinks Getränke
Bebidas Boissons Bibite

Months
Monate
Meses
Mois
Mesi
I
II
III
IV
V
VI

Months Monate
Meses Mois Mesi
VII
VIII
IX
X
XI
XII

Days Días	Tage Jours	Giorni				
S	**M**	**T**	**W**	**T**	**F**	**S**
S	M	D	M	D	F	S
D	L	M	M	J	V	S
D	L	M	M	J	V	S
D	L	M	M	G	V	S
1	2	3	4	5	6	7
8	9	10	11	12	13	14
15	16	17	18	19	20	21
22	23	24	25	26	27	28
29	30	31				

Time
Zeit
Tiempo
Temps
Tempo
A.M.
P.M.
1:15 P.M. = 13:15!
5:00 P.M. = 17:00!
4:30 P.M. = 16:30!
8:30 P.M. = 20:30!!!
11:10 P.M. = 23:10!!

Beauty Parlor / Schönheitssalon / Salón de Belleza / Salon de Beauté / Salone di Bellezza

Beauty Parlor Schönheitssalon
Salón de Belleza Salon de Beauté
Salone di Bellezza

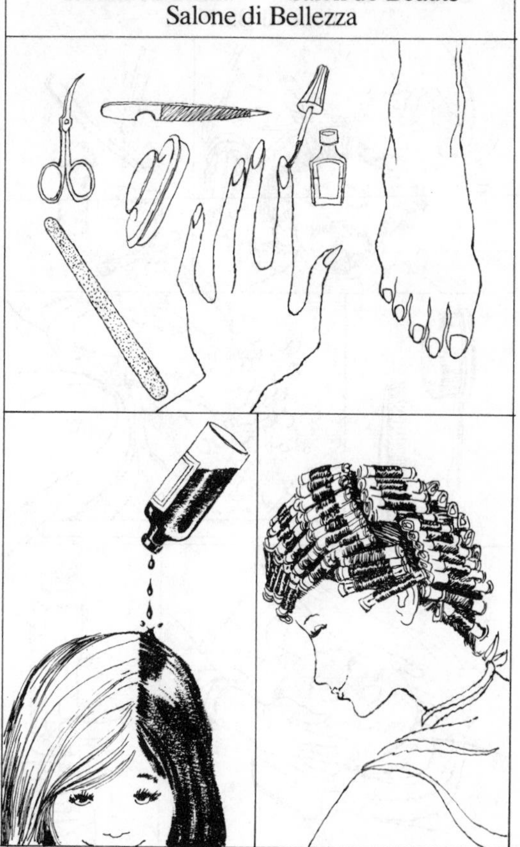

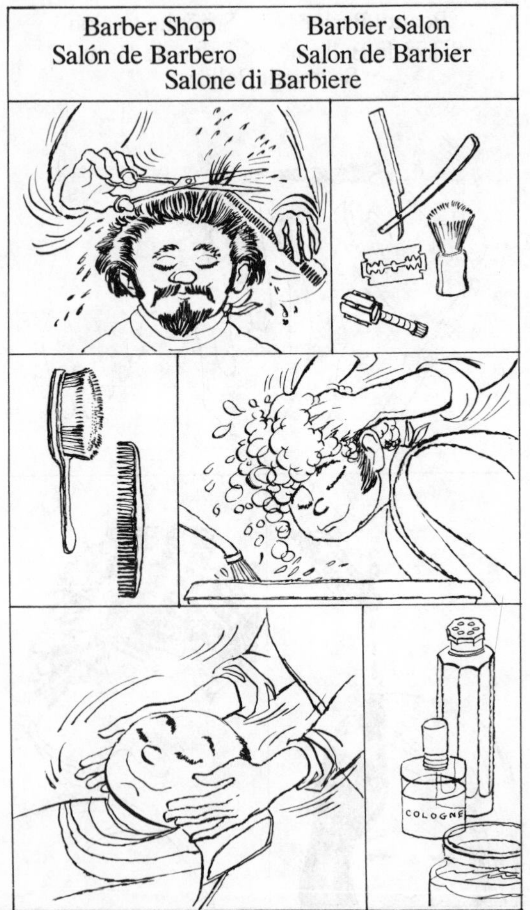
Barber Shop
Barbier Salon
Salón de Barbero
Salon de Barbier
Salone di Barbiere
COLOGNE

Barber Shop Barbier Salon
Salón de Barbero Salon de Barbier
Salone di Barbiere

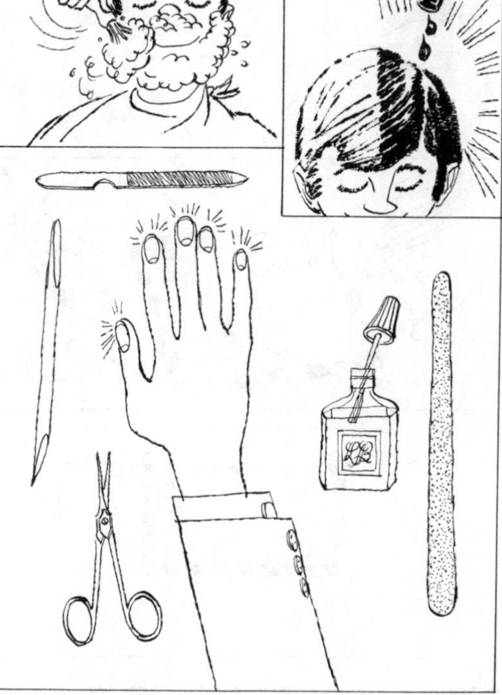

Mail
Post
Corréo
Courrier
Posta
AIR MAIL
PAR AVION

Mail Post
Corréo Courrier Posta

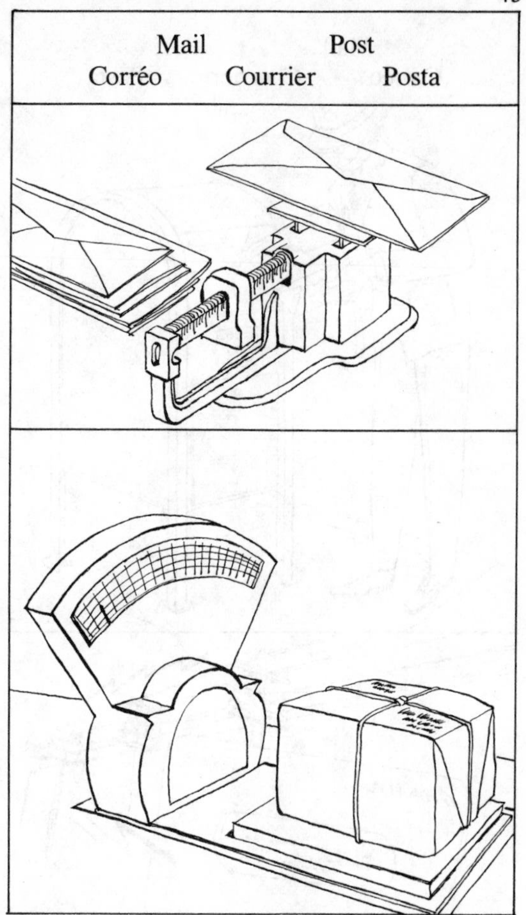

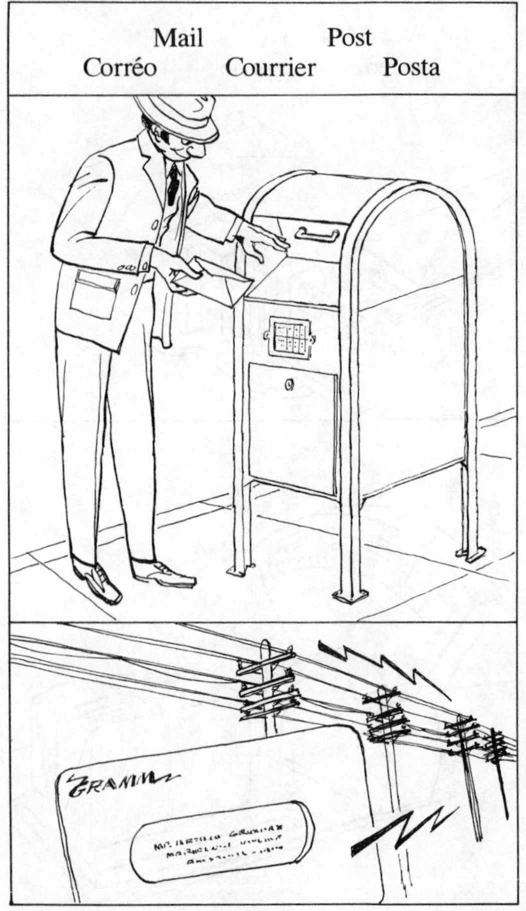
Mail Post
Corréo Courrier Posta

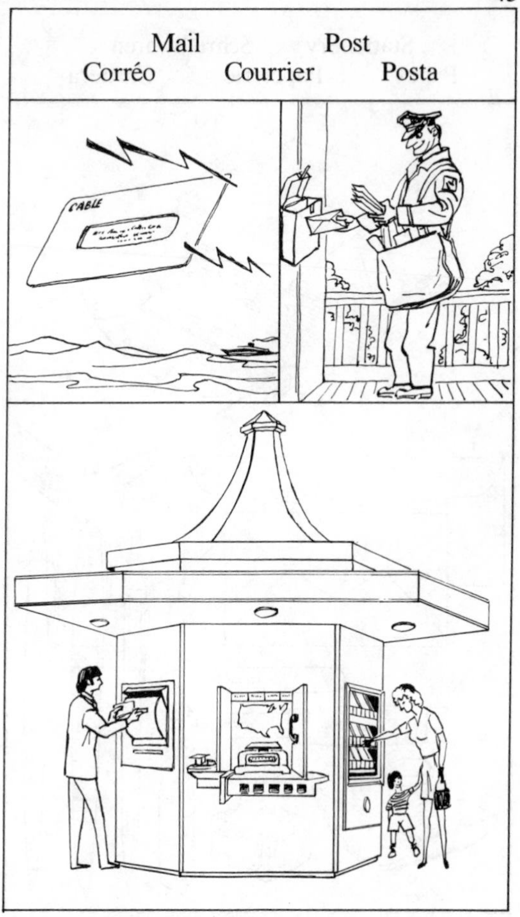
Mail Post
Corréo Courrier Posta
CABLE

Stationery Schreibwaren
Papel Papeterie Cartiera

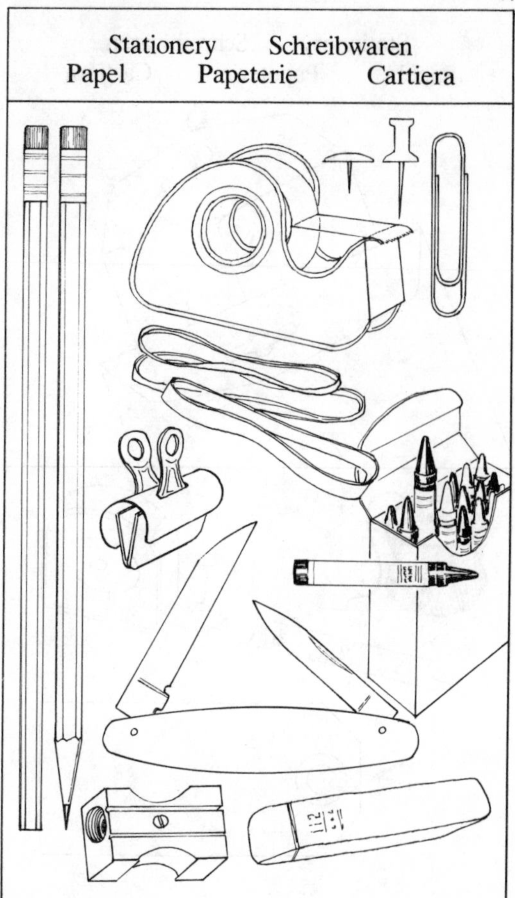

Stationery Schreibwaren
Papel Papeterie Cartiera

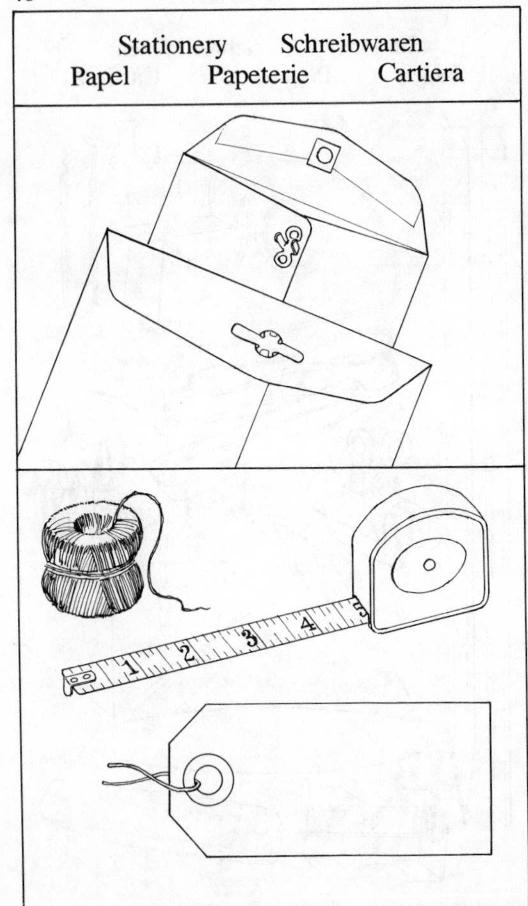
Stationery Schreibwaren
Papel Papeterie Cartiera
1
2
3
4
5

Stationery Schreibwaren Papel Papeterie Cartiera

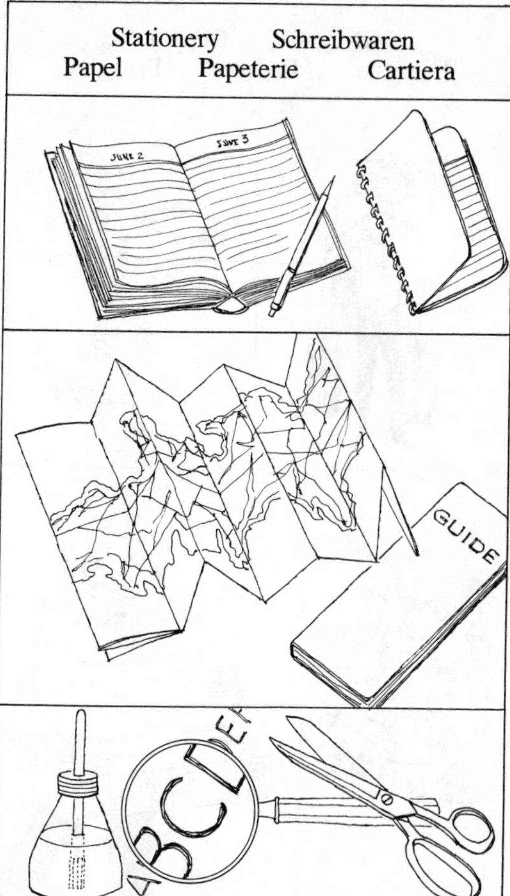

Baggage Gepäck
Equipaje Bagages Bagaglio
123
123
124

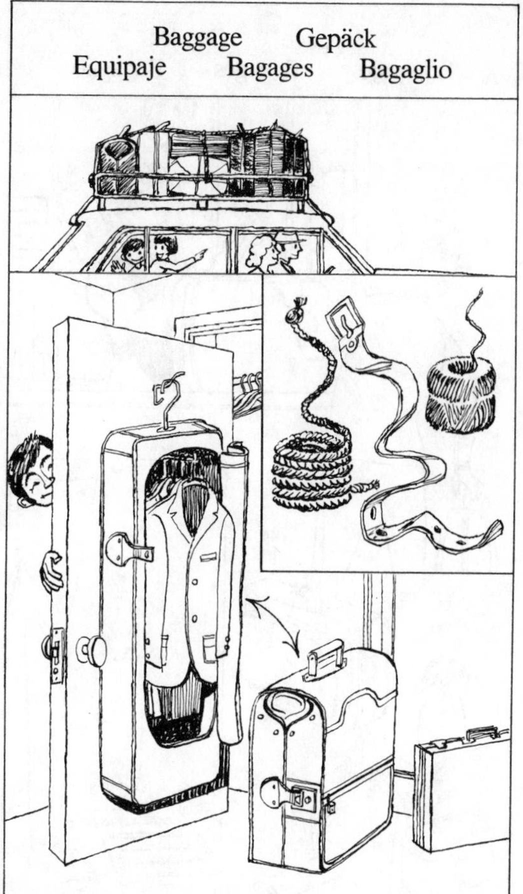
Baggage
Gepäck
Equipaje
Bagages
Bagaglio

Baggage Gepäck
Equipaje Bagages Bagaglio
12

Baggage Gepäck
Equipaje Bagages Bagaglio

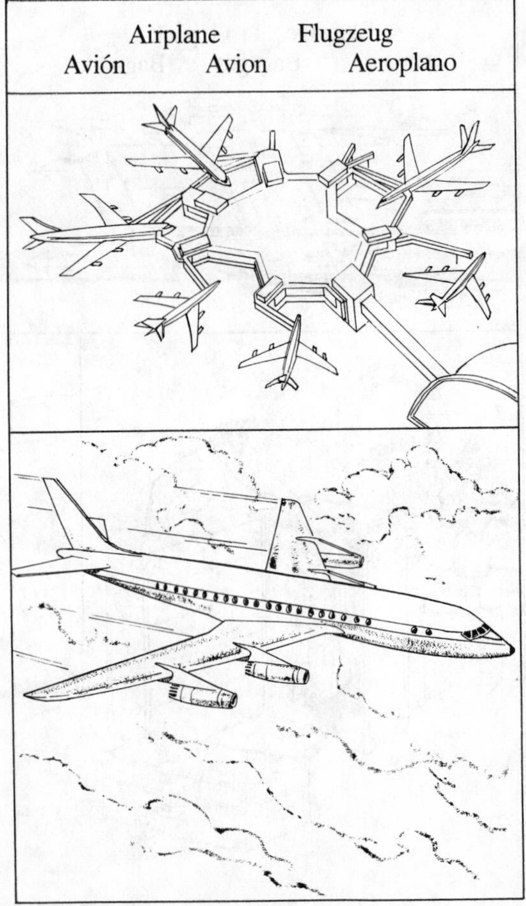
Airplane
Flugzeug
Avión
Avion
Aeroplano

Airplane Flugzeug
Avión Avion Aeroplano

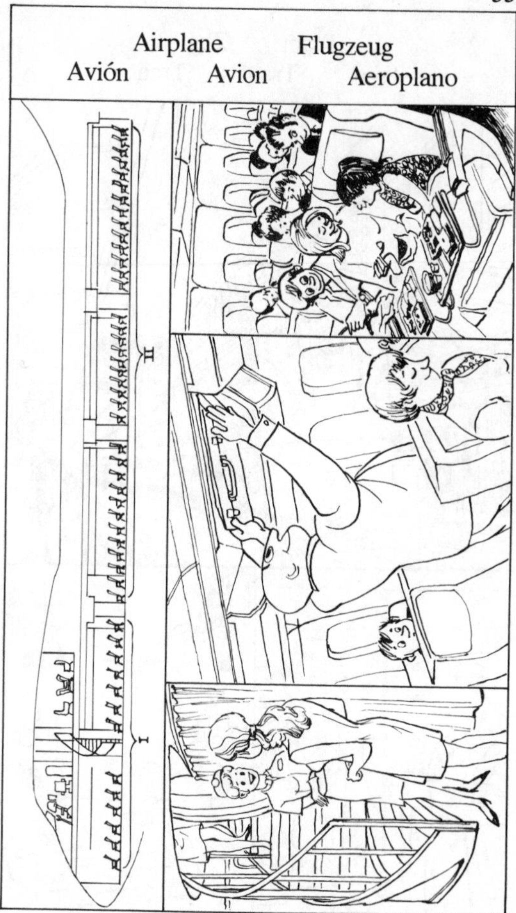

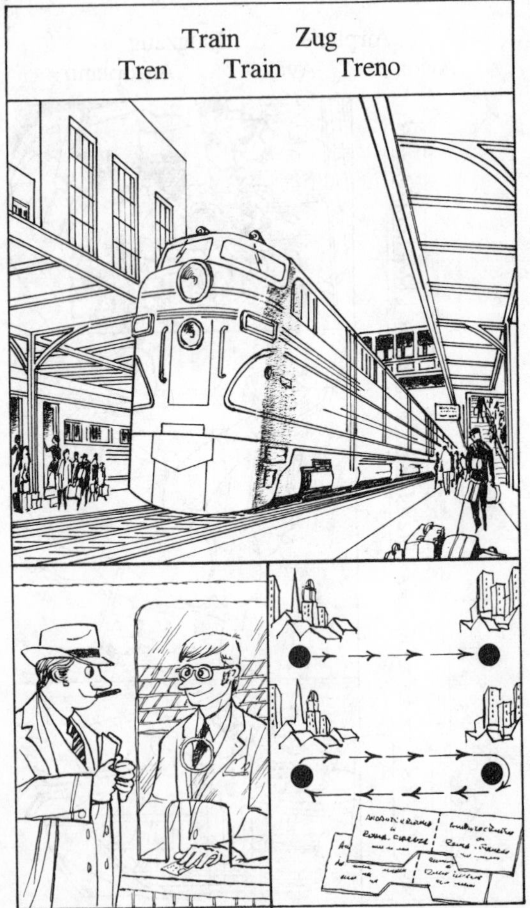
Train Zug
Tren Train Treno

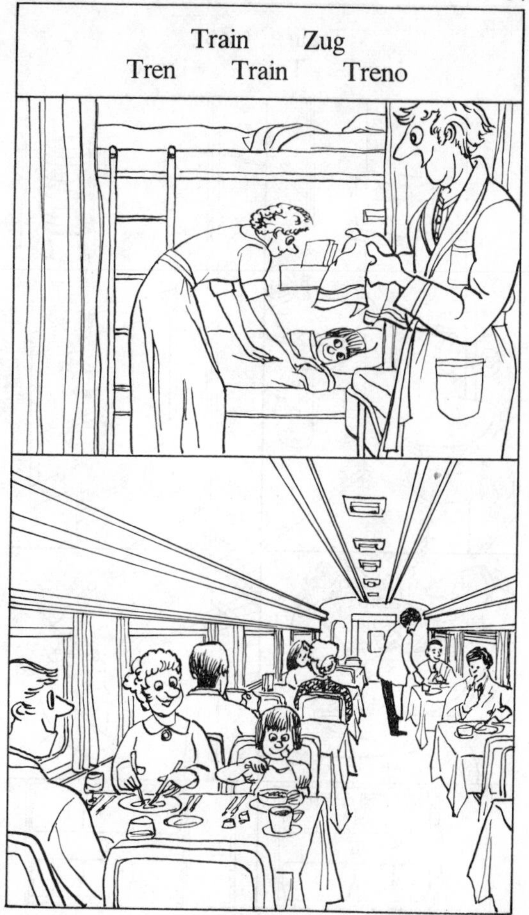
Train Zug
Tren Train Treno

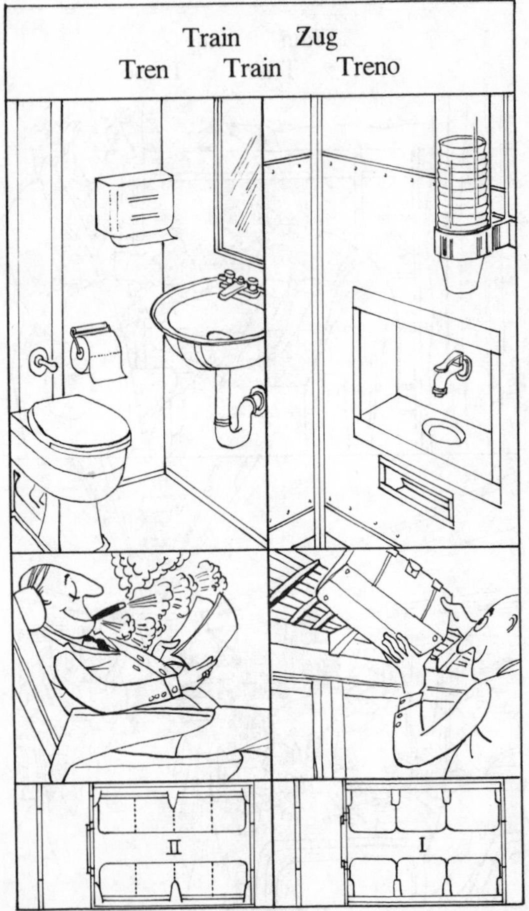
Train Zug
Tren Train Treno
II
I

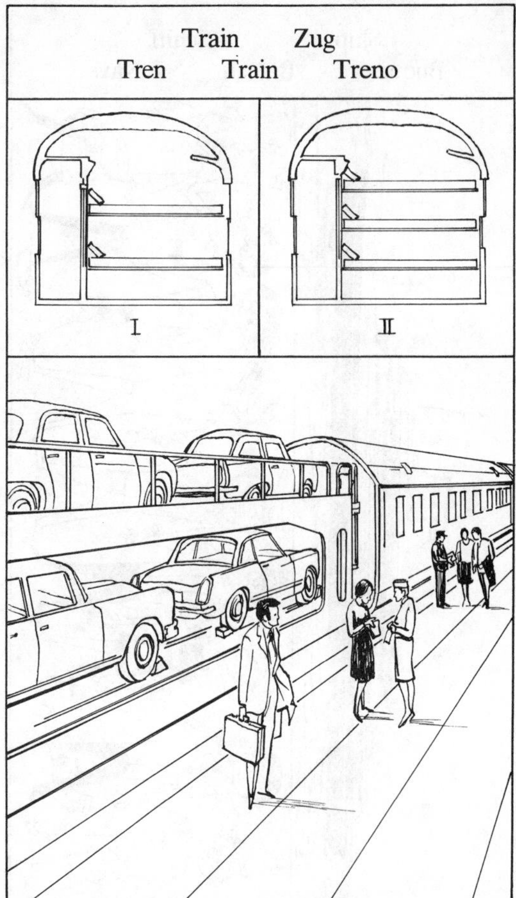
Train Zug
Tren Train Treno
I
II

Ship Schiff

Buque Bateau Nave

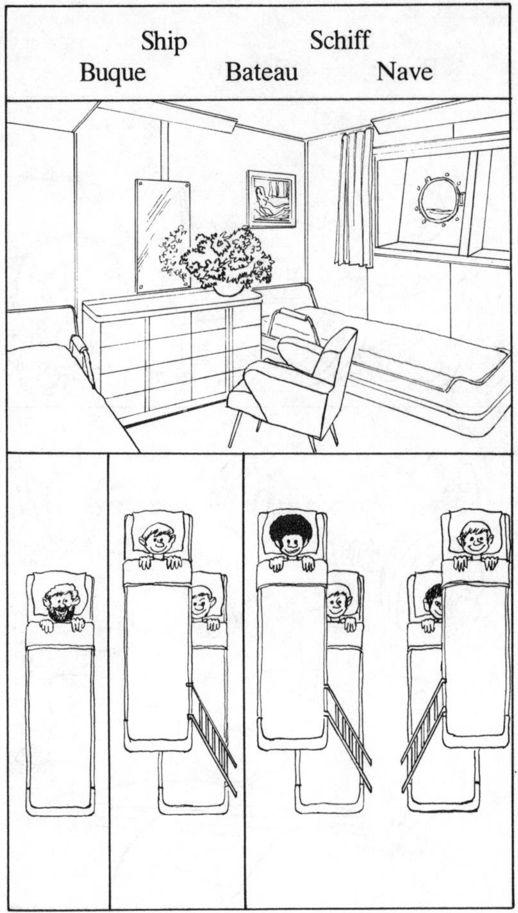
Ship
Schiff
Buque
Bateau
Nave

Ship
Schiff
Buque
Bateau
Nave

Ship
Schiff
Buque
Bateau
Nave
ZAP

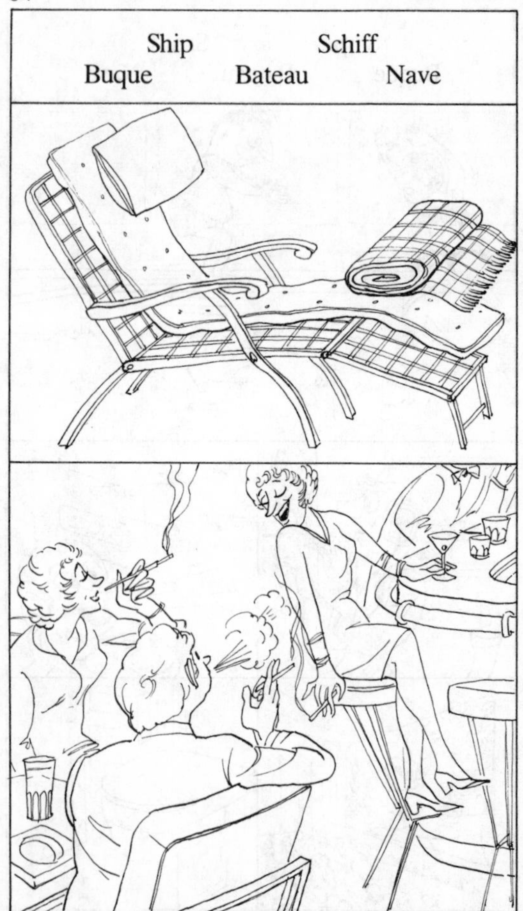
Ship
Schiff
Buque
Bateau
Nave

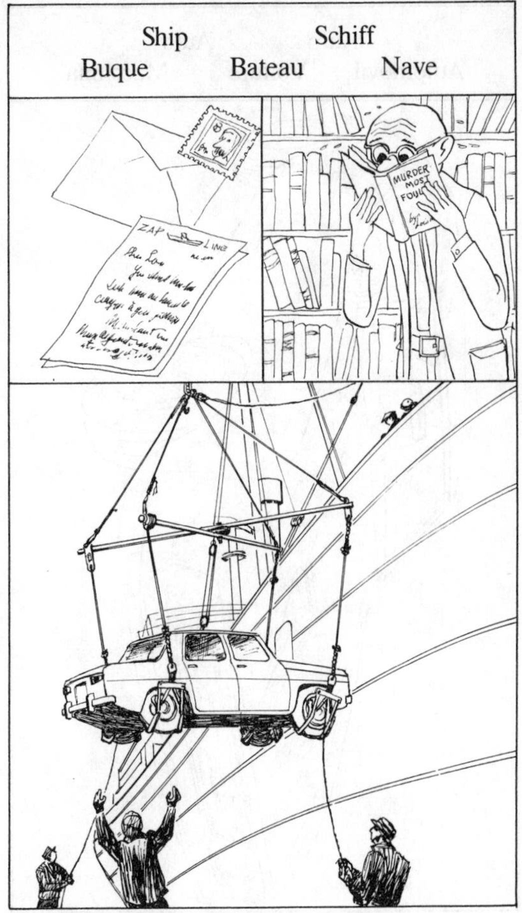
Ship
Schiff
Buque
Bateau
Nave
ZAP
LINE
MURDER MOST FOUL

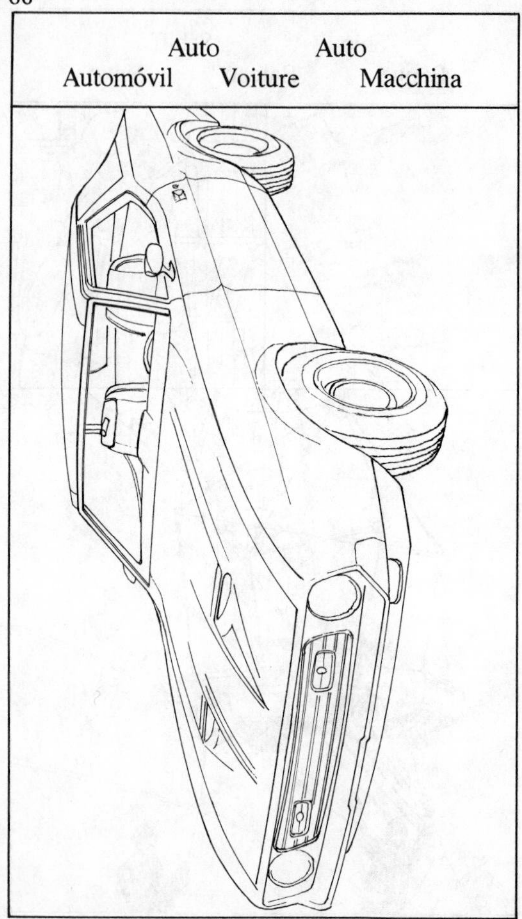
Auto Auto
Automóvil Voiture Macchina

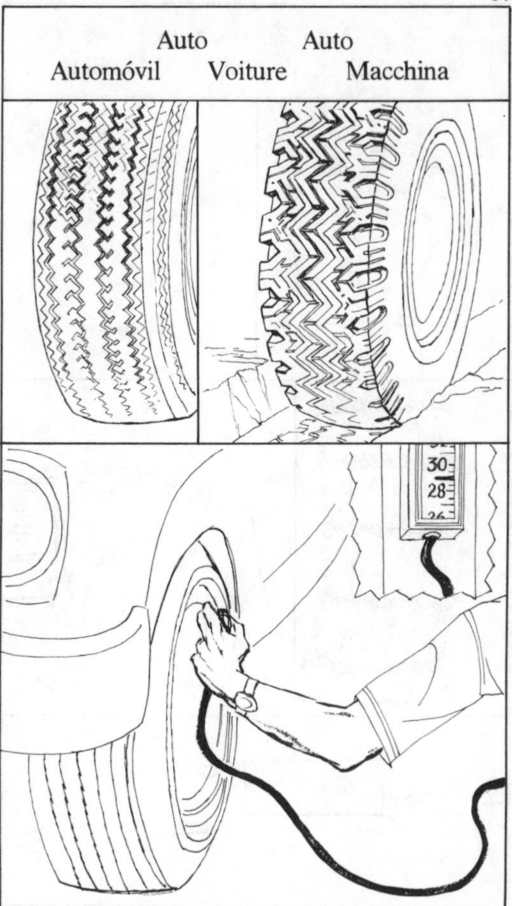
Auto Auto
Automóvil Voiture Macchina
30
28

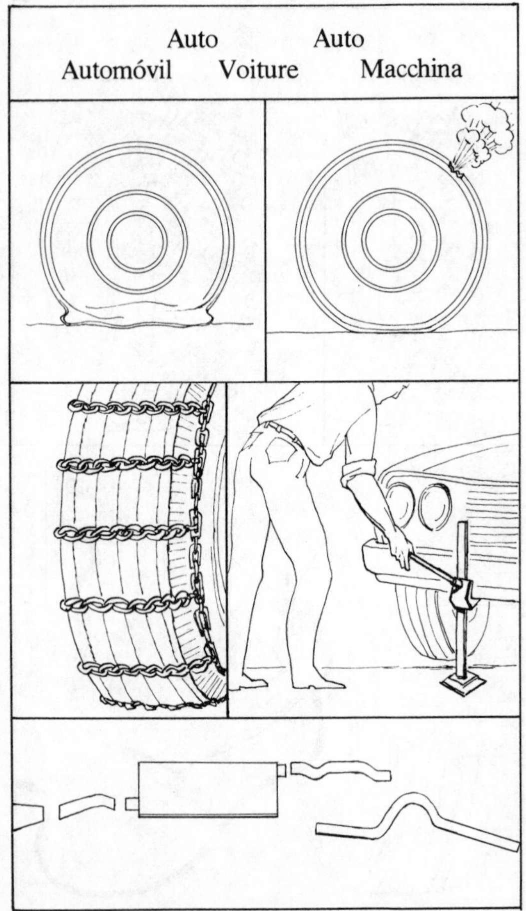
Auto Auto
Automóvil Voiture Macchina

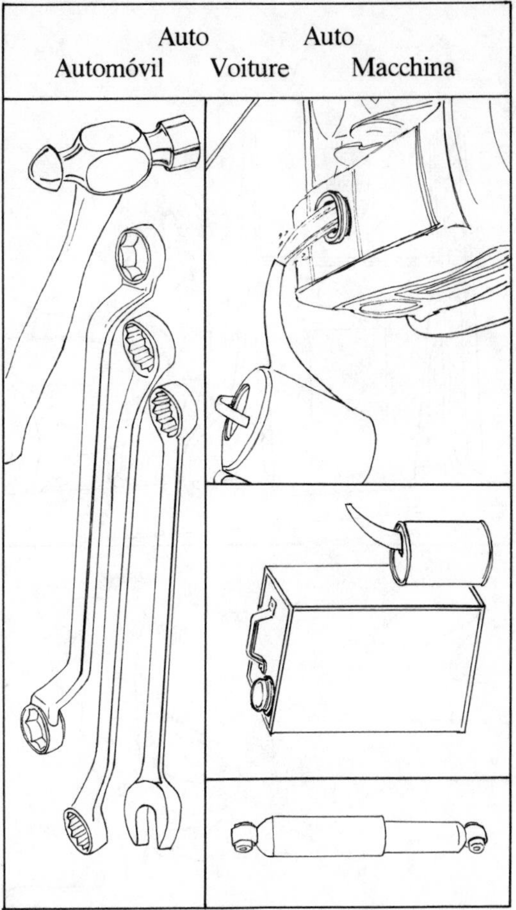
Auto Auto
Automóvil Voiture Macchina

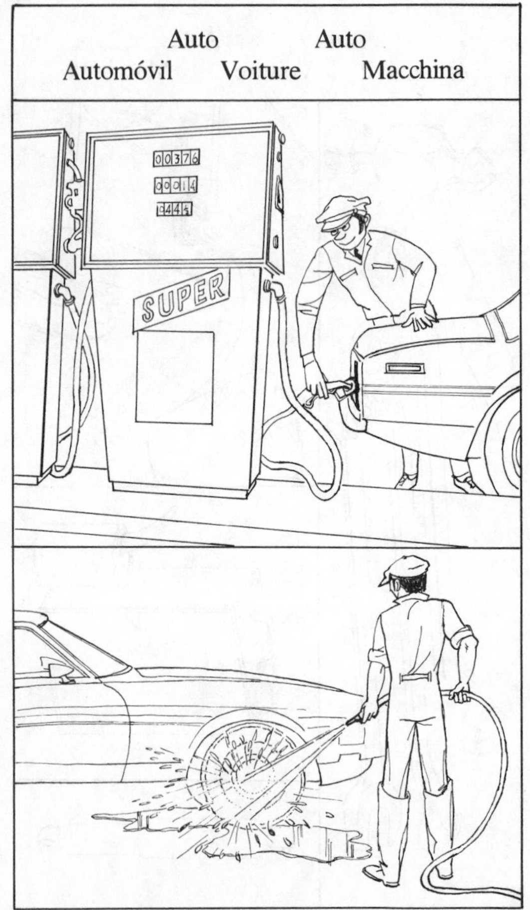
Auto Auto
Automóvil Voiture Macchina
00376
00014
SUPER

Auto Auto
Automóvil Voiture Macchina
EXIT
32 A

Auto Auto
Automóvil Voiture Macchina

Auto Auto
Automóvil Voiture Macchina

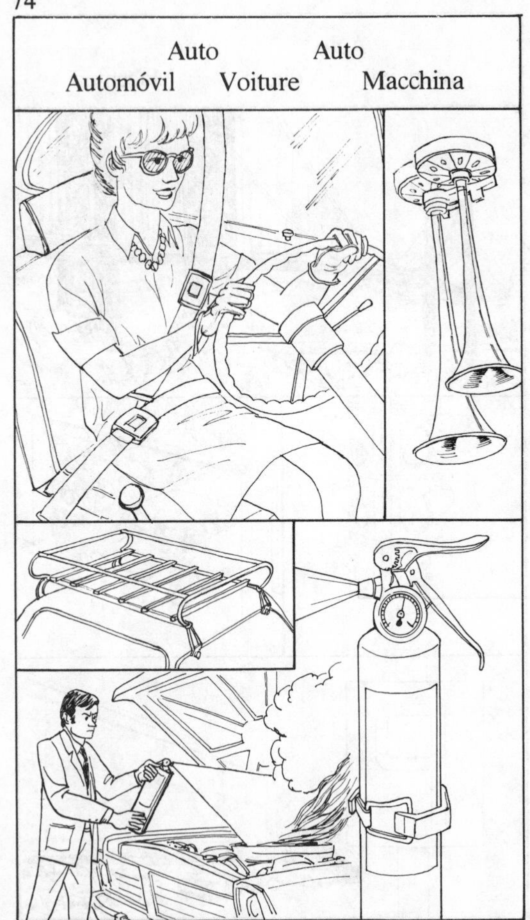
Auto Auto
Automóvil Voiture Macchina

Auto Auto
Automóvil Voiture Macchina

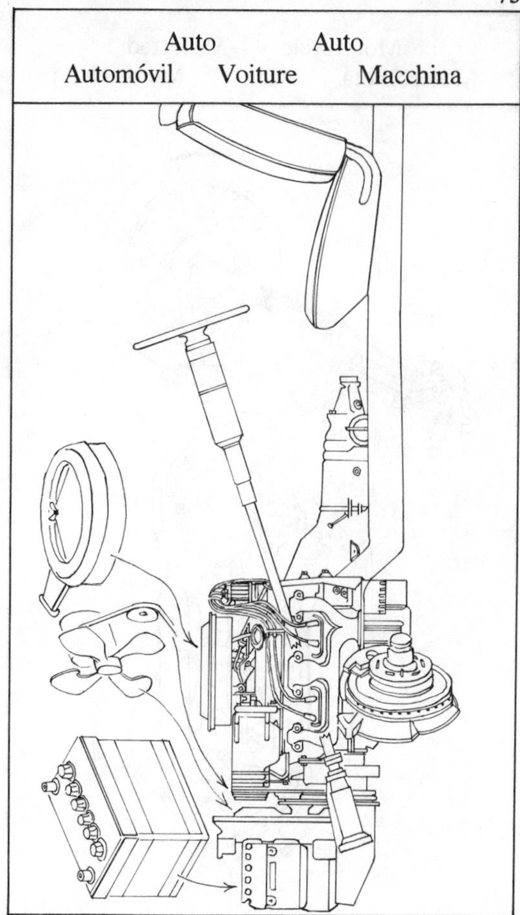

Motorcycle Motorrad
Motorcicleta Moto Motocicletta

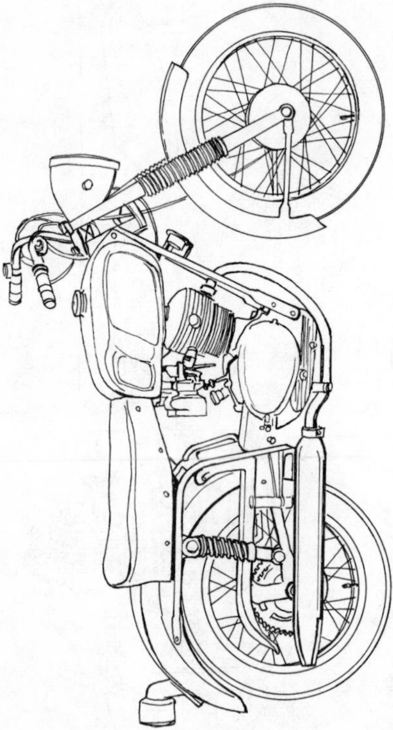

Motorcycle Motorrad
Motorcicleta Moto Motocicletta

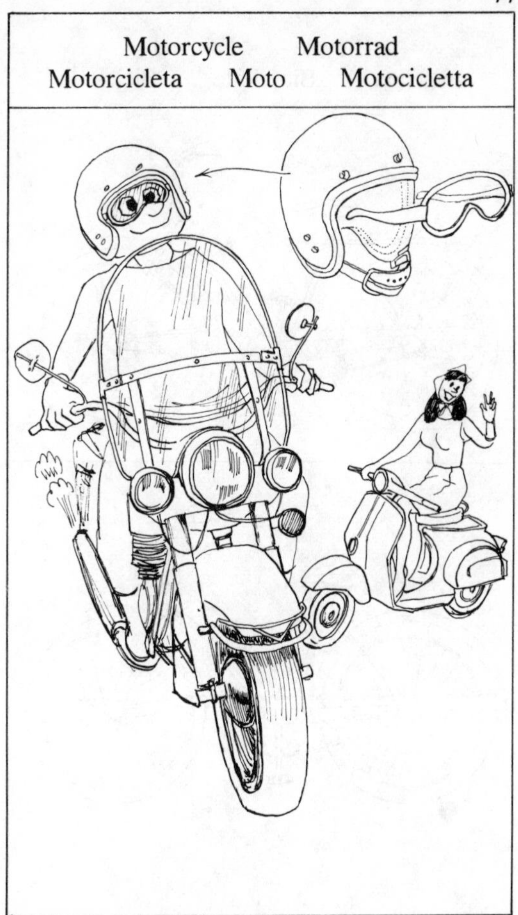

Bicycle Fahrrad
Bicicleta Bicyclette Bicicletta

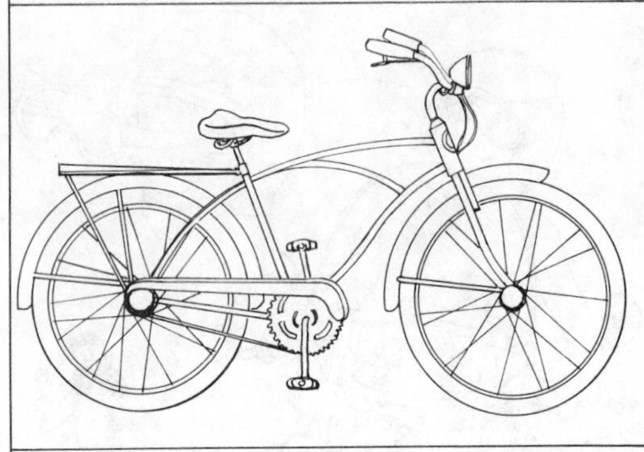

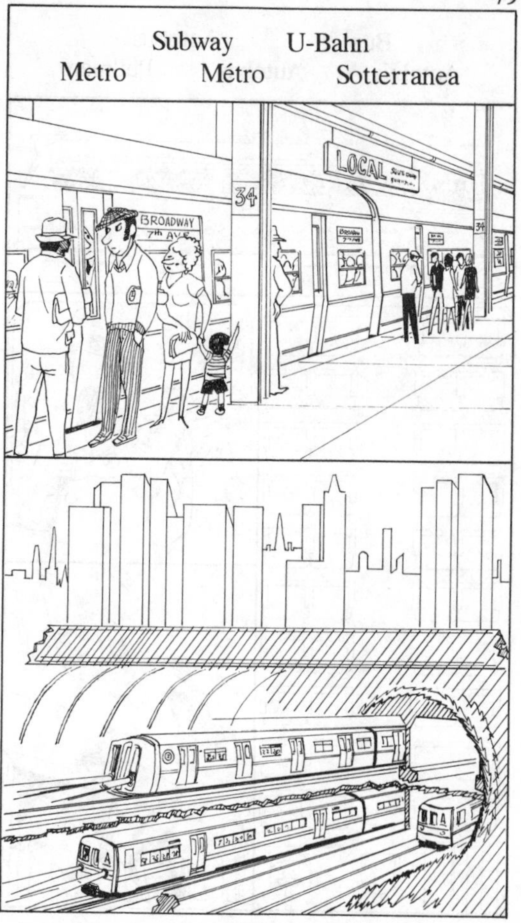
Subway
U-Bahn
Metro
Métro
Sotterranea
LOCAL
BROADWAY
7th AVE
34
34
A
A

Bus
Autobus
Autobús
Autobus
Pullman

Transportation Beforderung
Transportación Transport Trasporto
134
VICTORIA
TAXI

Transportation Beforderung Transportación Transport Trasporto

Transportation Beforderung
Transportación Transport Trasporto

Transportation Beforderung Transportación Transport Trasporto

Transportation Beforderung
Transportación Transport Trasporto

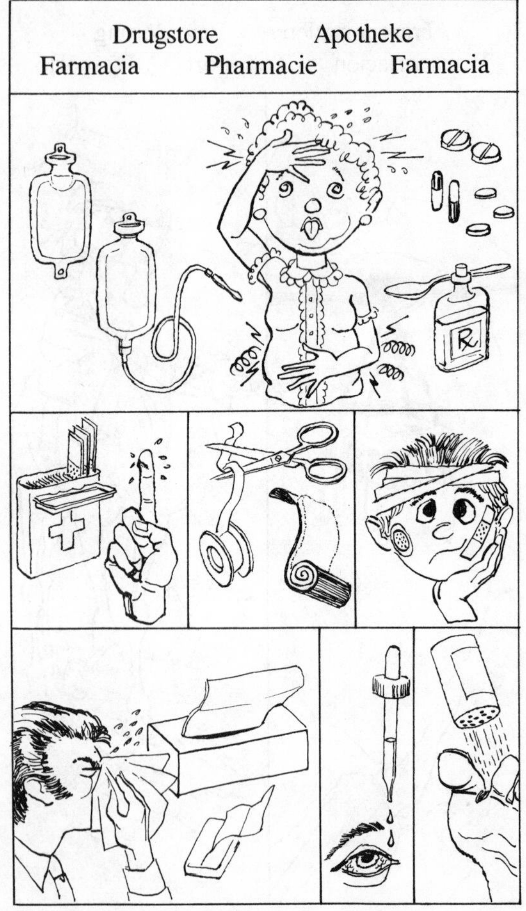
Drugstore Apotheke
Farmacia Pharmacie Farmacia

Drugstore
Apotheke
Farmacia
Pharmacie
Farmacia

Drugstore Apotheke
Farmacia Pharmacie Farmacia

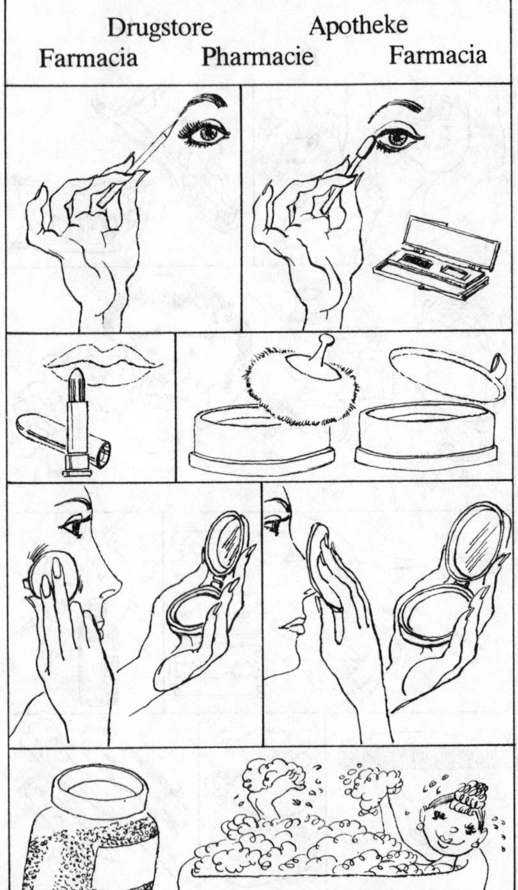

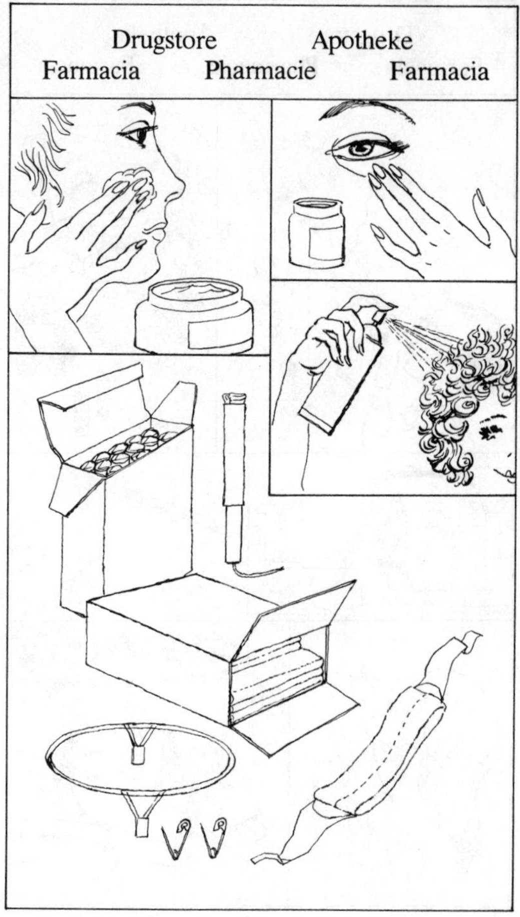
Drugstore
Apotheke
Farmacia
Pharmacie
Farmacia

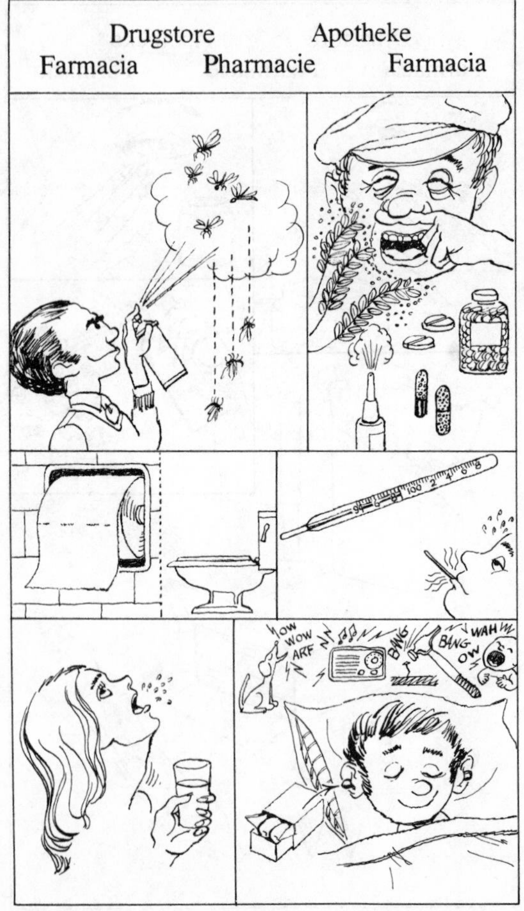
Drugstore
Apotheke
Farmacia
Pharmacie
Farmacia
WOW
ARF
BANG
BANG
OW
WAH

Drugstore
Apotheke
Farmacia
Pharmacie
Farmacia
1
!?
2
3
!!??
4

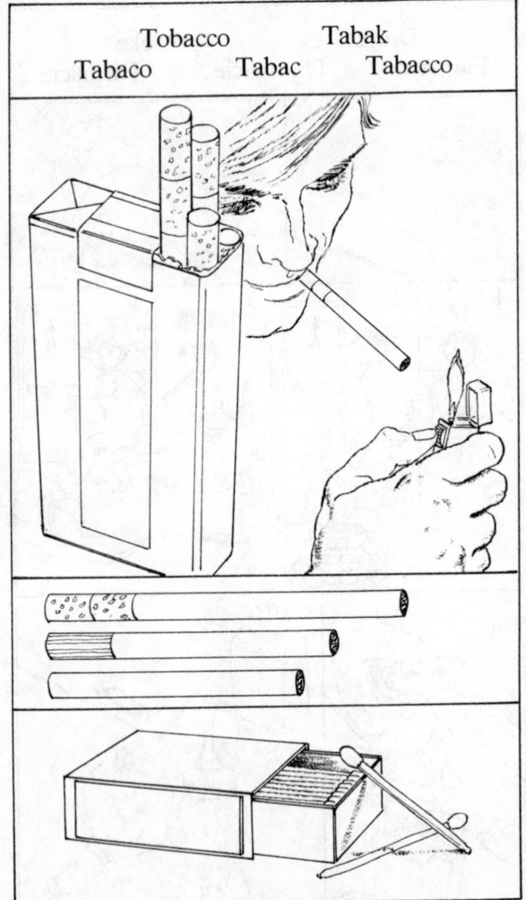
Tobacco
Tabak
Tabaco
Tabac
Tabacco

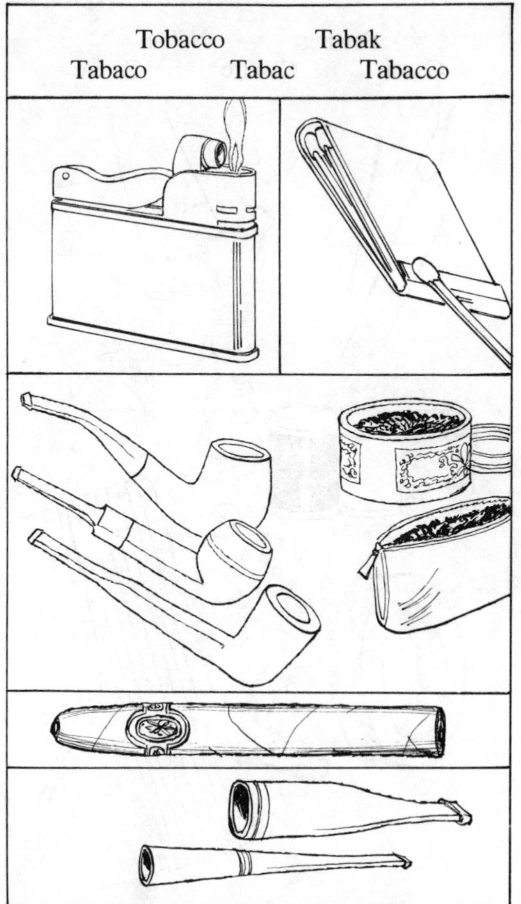
Tobacco Tabak
Tabaco Tabac Tabacco

Sewing Nähen
Coser Coudre Cucire

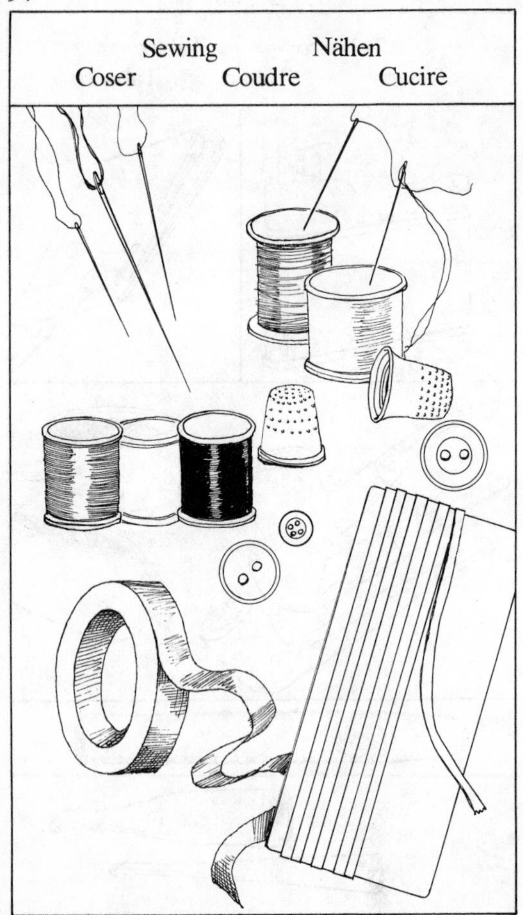

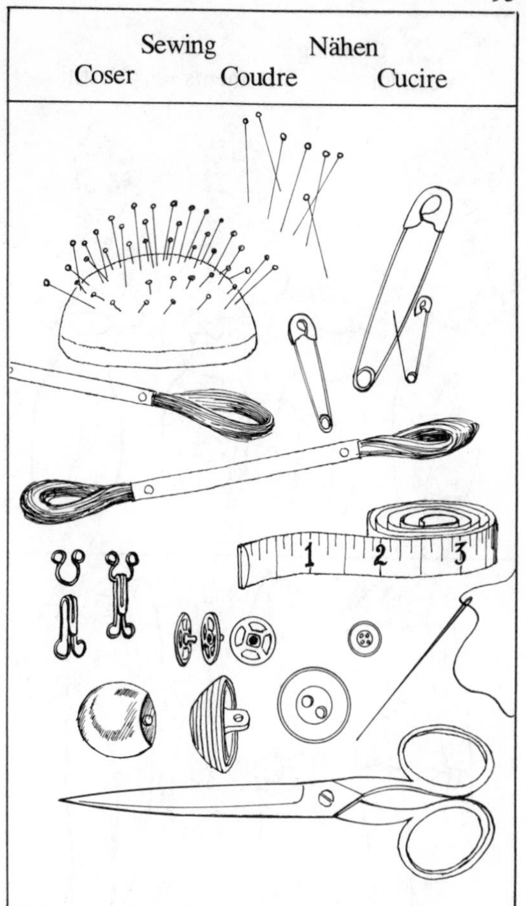
Sewing Nähen
Coser Coudre Cucire
1
2
3

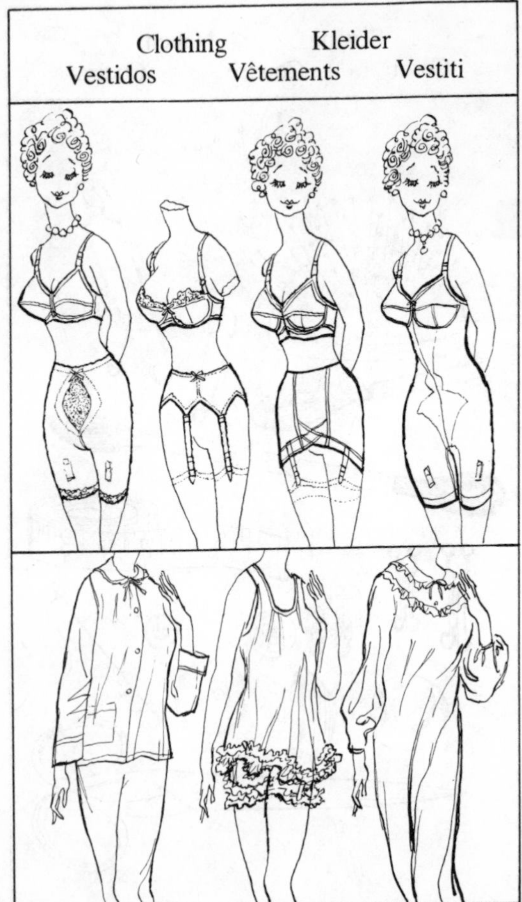
Clothing
Kleider
Vestidos
Vêtements
Vestiti

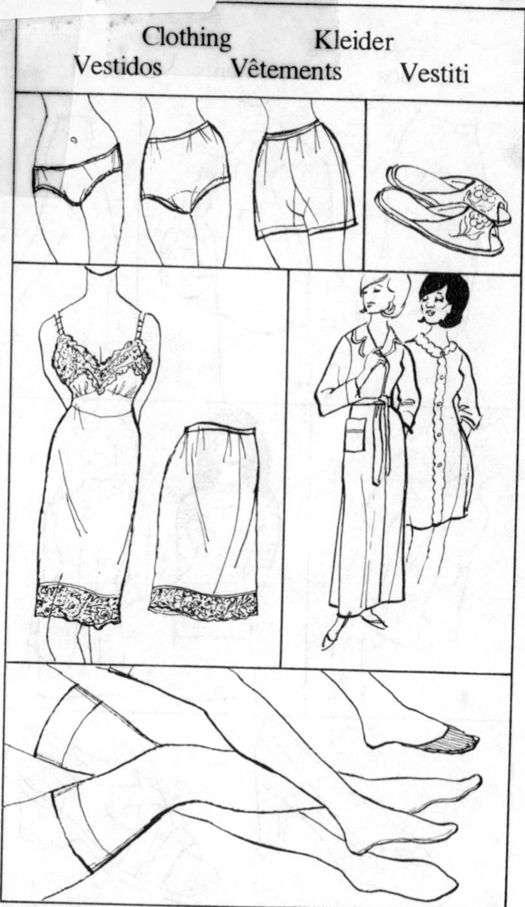
Clothing Kleider
Vestidos Vêtements Vestiti

Clothing
Kleider
Vestidos
Vêtements
Vestiti

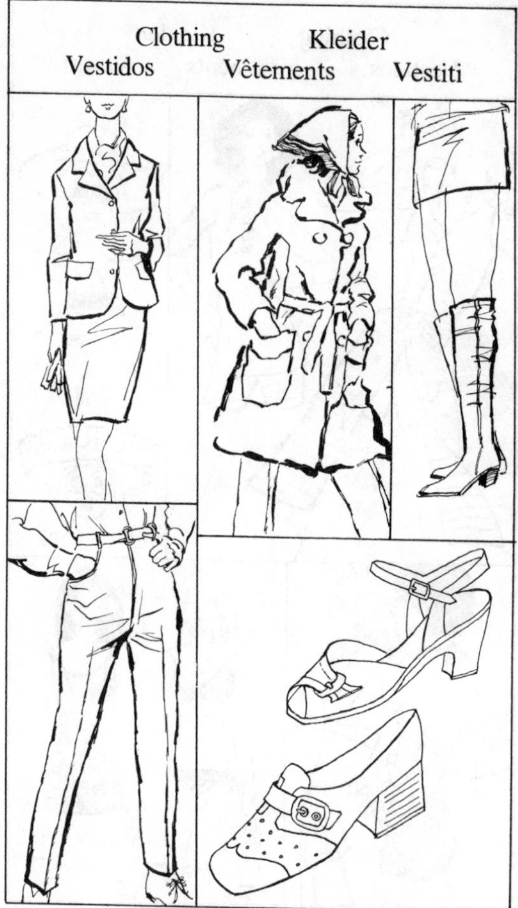
Clothing
Kleider
Vestidos
Vêtements
Vestiti

Clothing Kleider
Vestidos Vêtements Vestiti

Clothing
Kleider
Vestidos
Vêtements
Vestiti

Clothing Kleider
Vestidos Vêtements Vestiti

Clothing Kleider
Vestidos Vêtements Vestiti

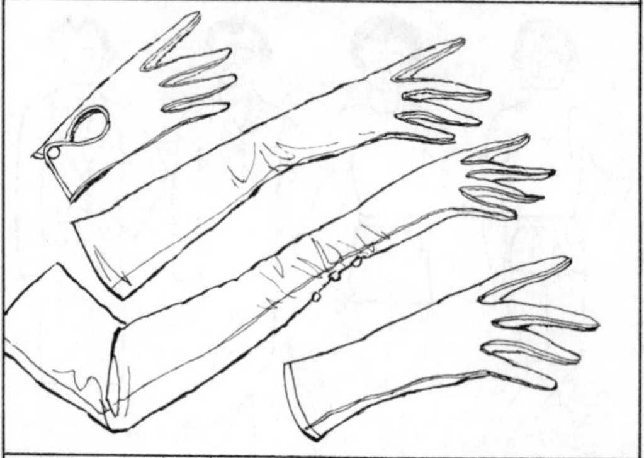

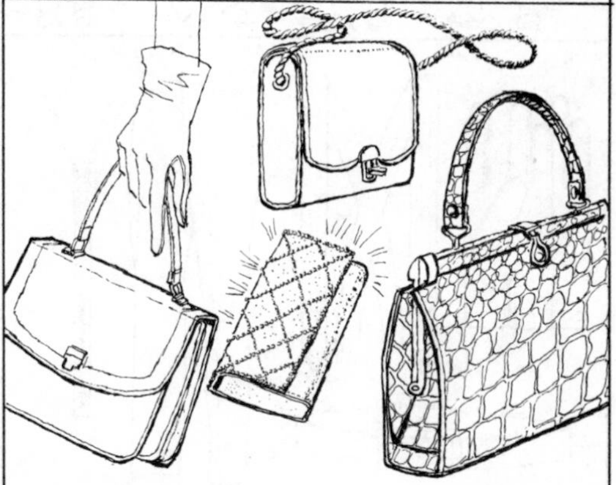

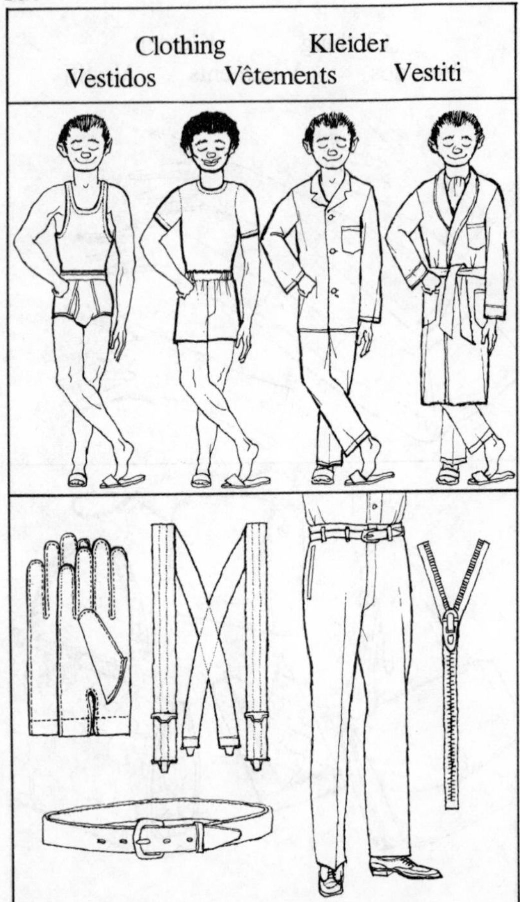
Clothing
Kleider
Vestidos
Vêtements
Vestiti

Clothing Kleider
Vestidos Vêtements Vestiti

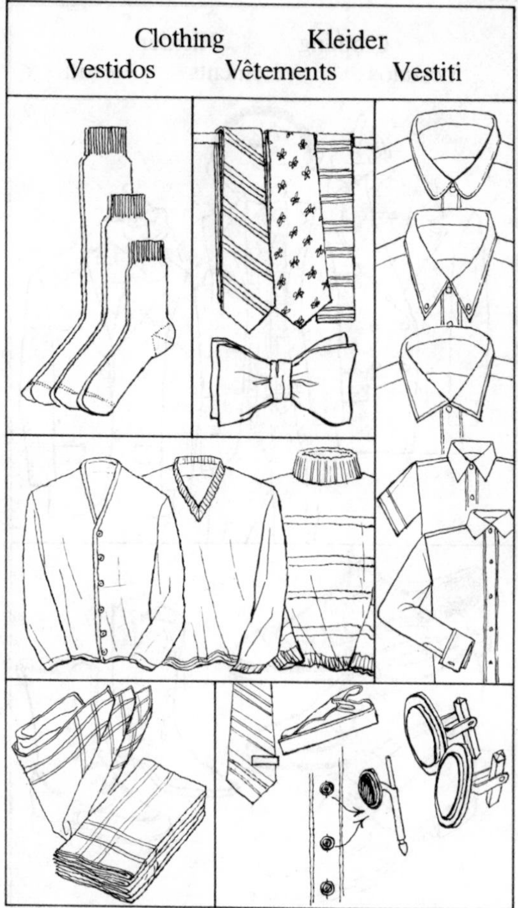

Clothing Kleider
Vestidos Vêtements Vestiti

Clothing
Kleider
Vestidos
Vêtements
Vestiti

Clothing Kleider
Vestidos Vêtements Vestiti

Clothing
Kleider
Vestidos
Vêtements
Vestiti

Gifts Geschenke
Regalos Cadeaux Regali

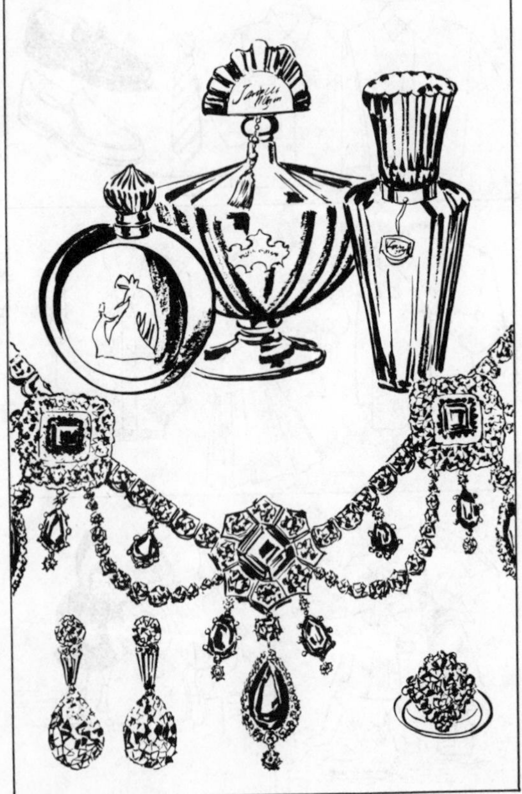

Gifts Geschenke
Regalos Cadeaux Regali

Gifts Geschenke
Regalos Cadeaux Regali

Gifts Geschenke
Regalos Cadeaux Regali

Gifts Geschenke
Regalos Cadeaux Regali

Gifts Geschenke
Regalos Cadeaux Regali

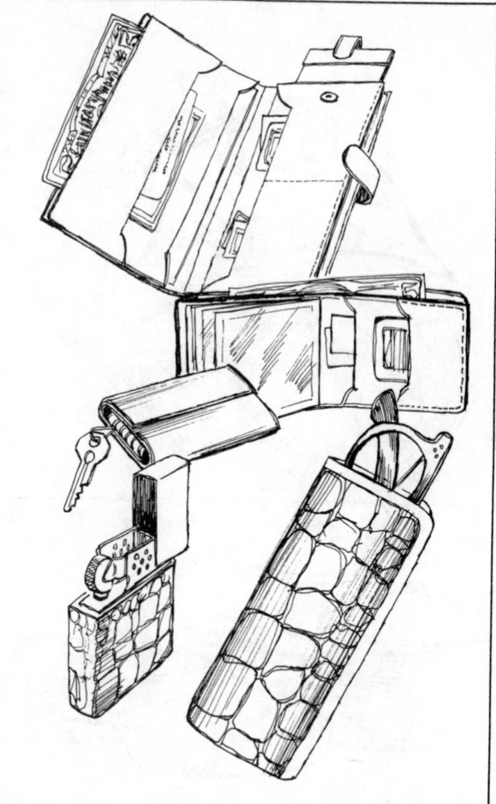

Gifts Geschenke Regalos Cadeaux Regali

Gifts Geschenke
Regalos Cadeaux Regali

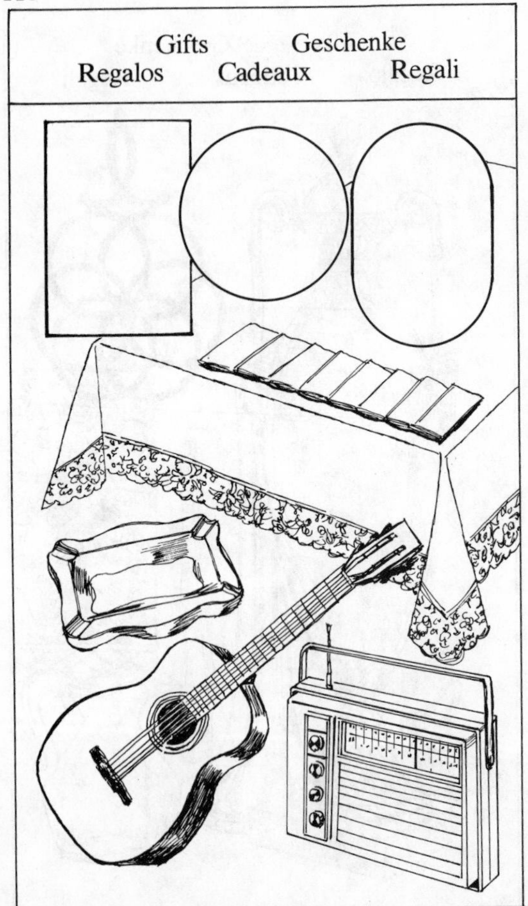
Gifts
Geschenke
Regalos
Cadeaux
Regali

Gifts Geschenke
Regalos Cadeaux Regali

Camera Kamera Cámera
Appareil Photographique
Macchina Fotografica

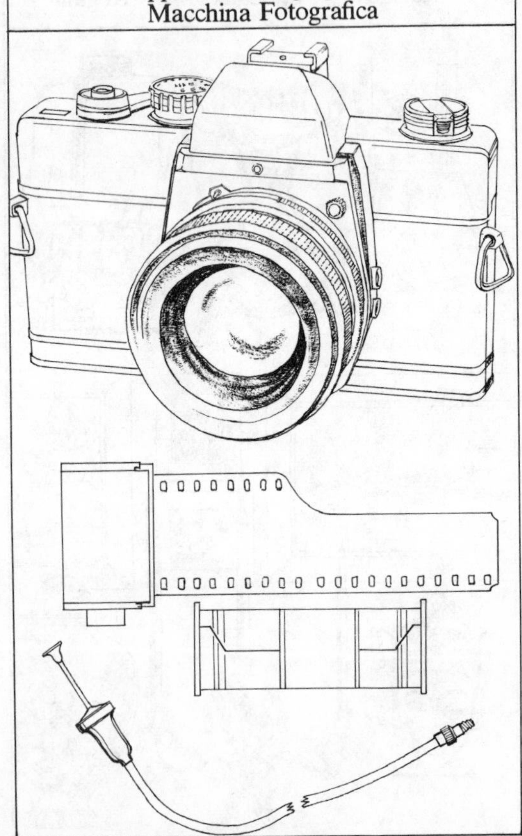

Camera Kamera Cámera
Appareil Photographique
Macchina Fotografica

Camera Kamera Cámera
Appareil Photographique
Macchina Fotografica

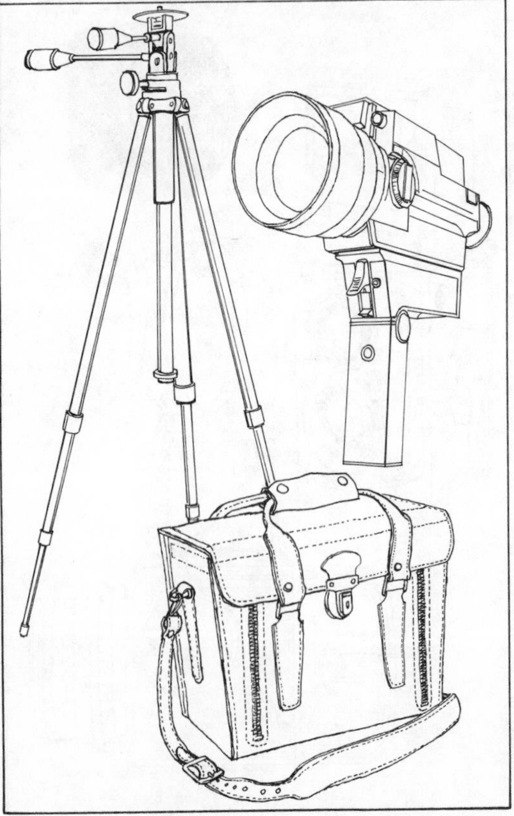

Camera Kamera Cámera
Appareil Photographique
Macchina Fotografica

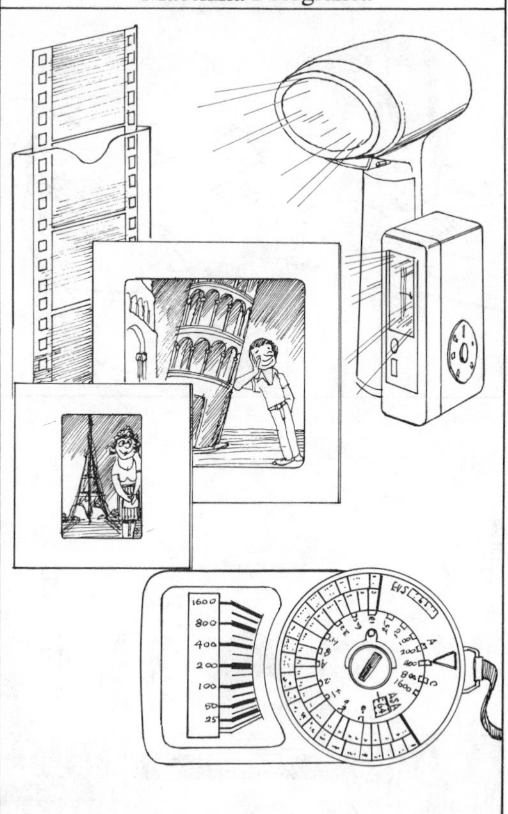

Sightseeing   Besuchen von Sehenswürdigkeiten
Visita de Puntos de Interés
Tourisme   Girare per Vedere le Curiosità

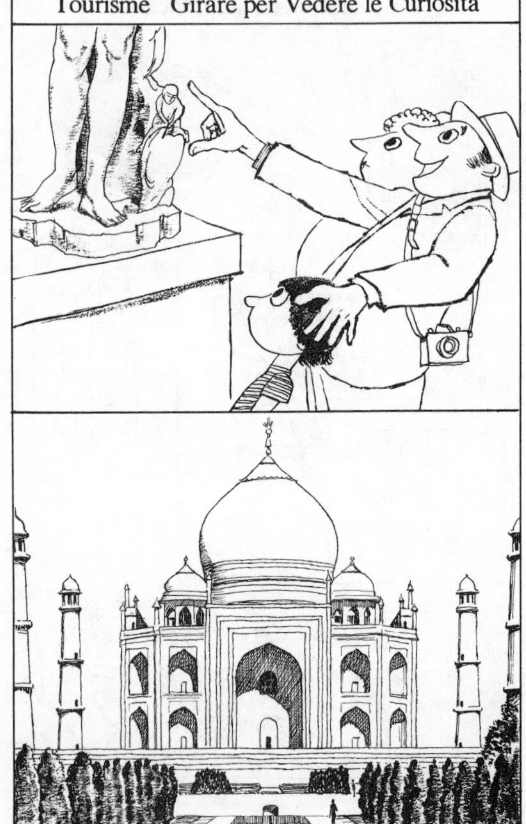

Sightseeing Besuchen von Sehenswürdigkeiten Visita de Puntos de Interés Tourisme Girare per Vedere le Curiosità

Sightseeing   Besuchen von Sehenswürdigkeiten
Visita de Puntos de Interés
Tourisme   Girare per Vedere le Curiosità

Sightseeing Besuchen von Sehenswürdigkeiten Visita de Puntos de Interés Tourisme Girare per Vedere le Curiosità

Amusements Unterhaltungen
Diversiones Divertissements Divertimenti

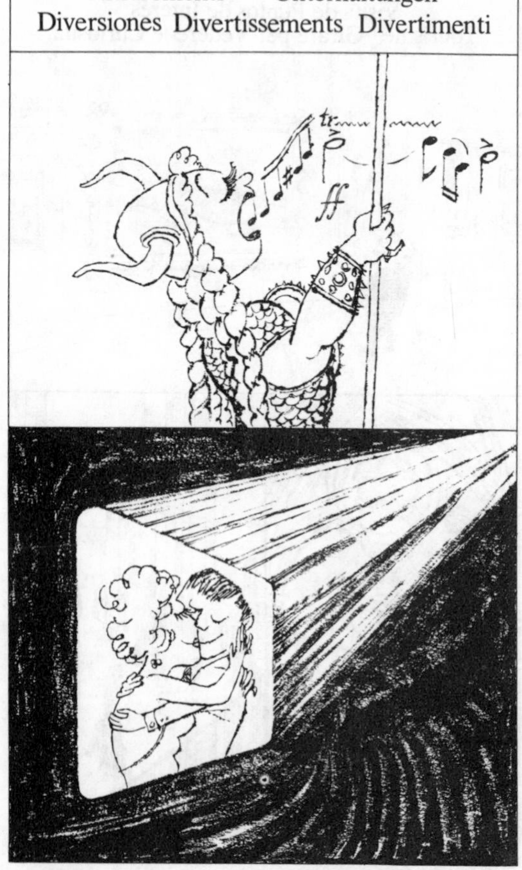

Amusements Unterhaltungen Diversiones Divertissements Divertimenti

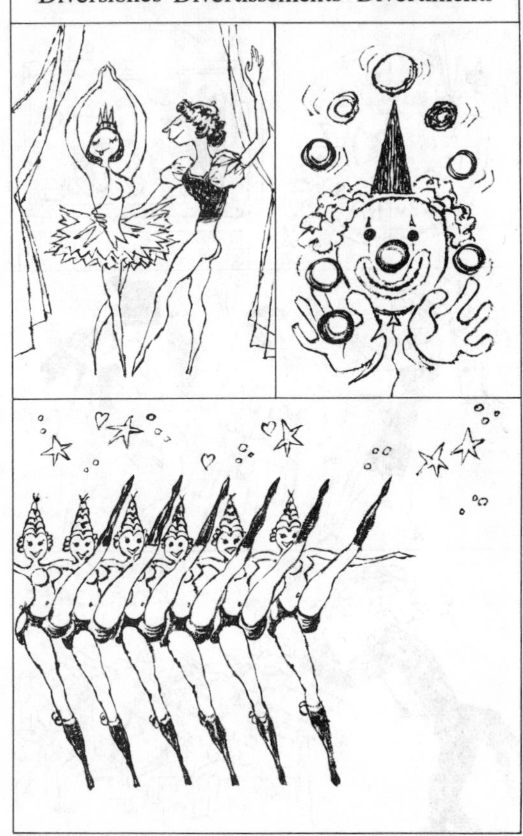

Amusements Unterhaltungen Diversiónes Divertissements Divertimenti

Amusements Unterhaltungen Diversiónes Divertissements Divertimenti

Games Spiele
Juegos Jeux Giochi

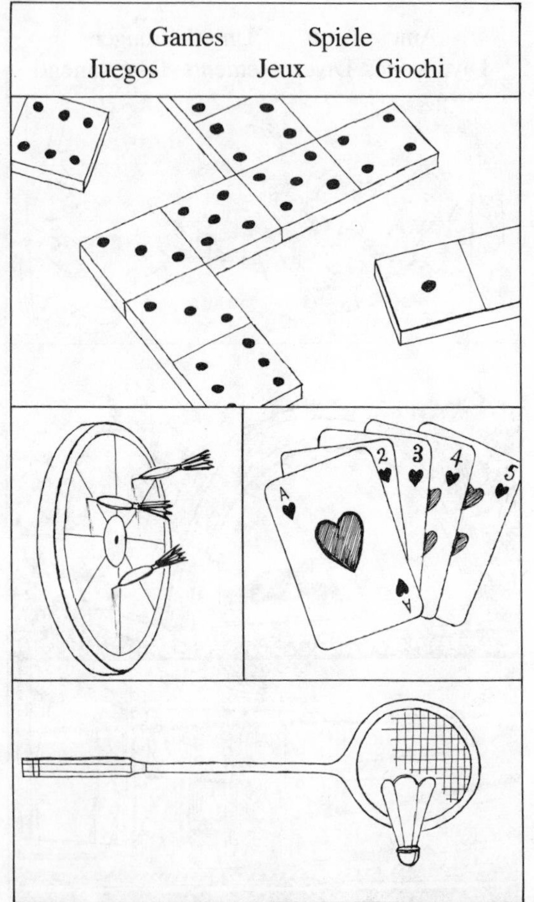

Games Spiele
Juegos Jeux Giochi

Games Spiele
Juegos Jeux Giochi

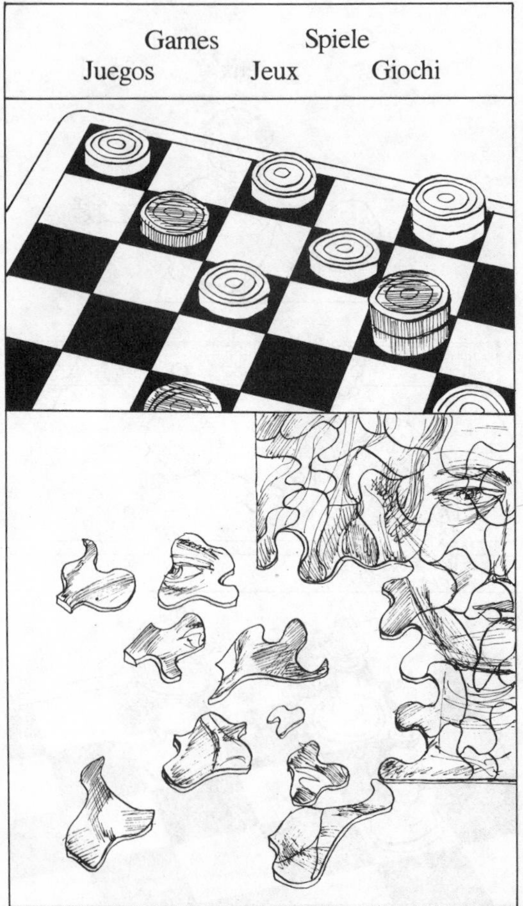

Sports
Sport
Depores
Spors
Sport

Sports Sport
Deportes Sports Sport

Sports Sport
Deportes Sports Sport

Sports Sport
Deportes Sports Sport

Sports Sport
Deportes Sports Sport

Sports Sport
Deportes Sports Sport
5
4

Sports Sport
Deportes Sports Sport

Sports Sport
Deportes Sports Sport

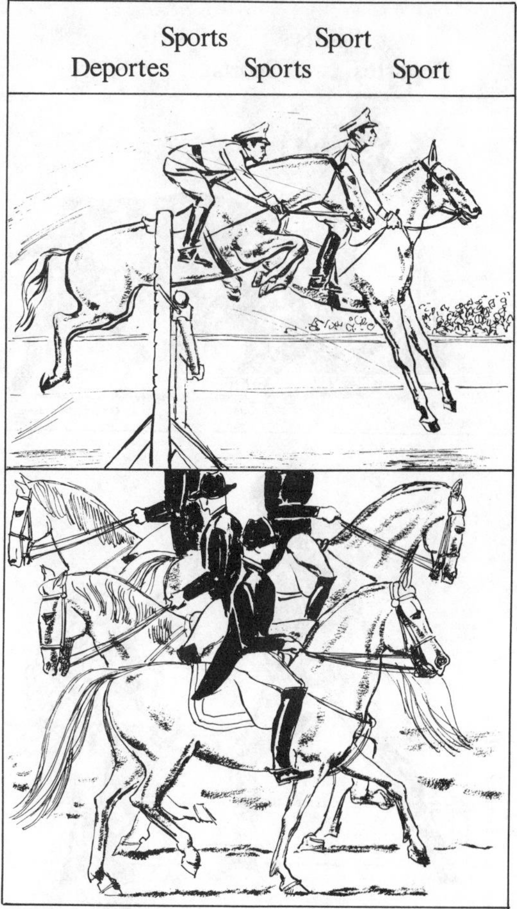
Sports
Sport
Deportes
Sports
Sport

Sports Sport
Deportes Sports Sport

Sports Sport
Deportes Sports Sport

Sports Sport
Deportes Sports Sport

Sports Sport
Deportes Sports Sport

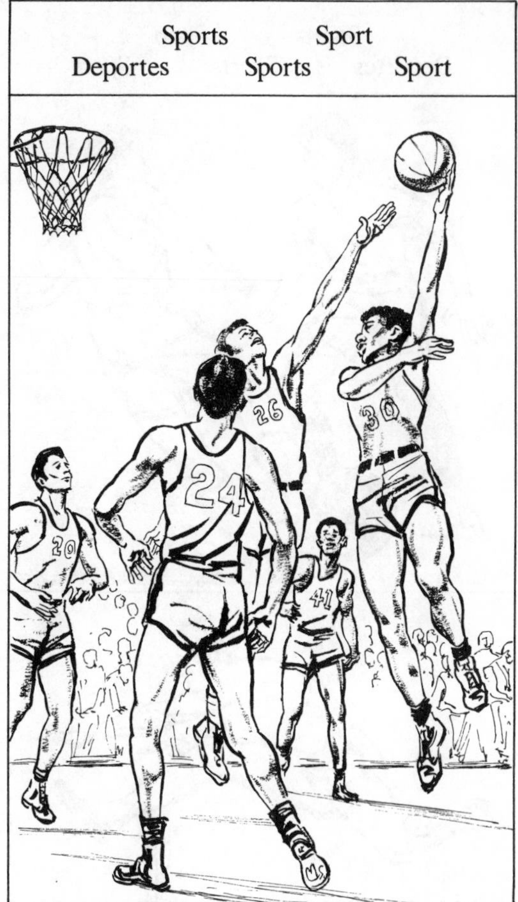

Sports Sport
Deportes Sports Sport

Sports Sport
Deportes Sports Sport

Camping Camping
Camping Camping Campeggio

Camping Camping
Camping Camping Campeggio

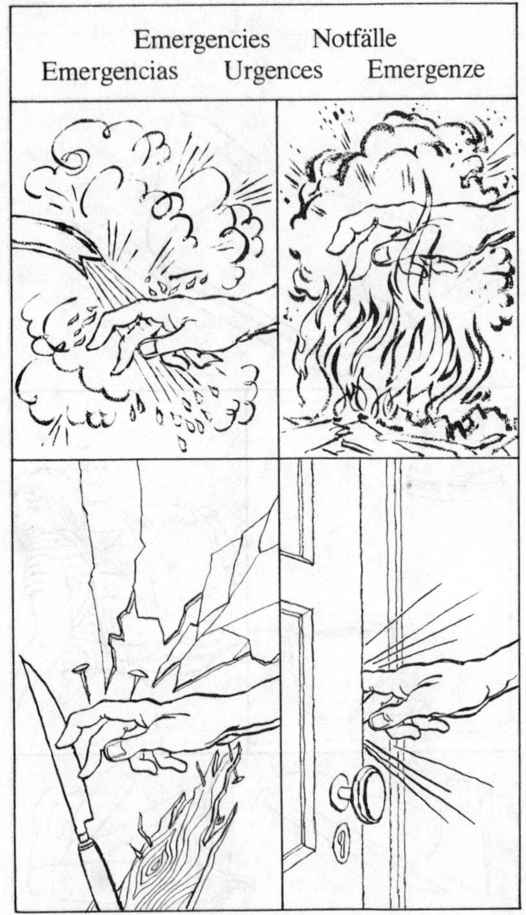
Emergencies Notfälle
Emergencias Urgences Emergenze

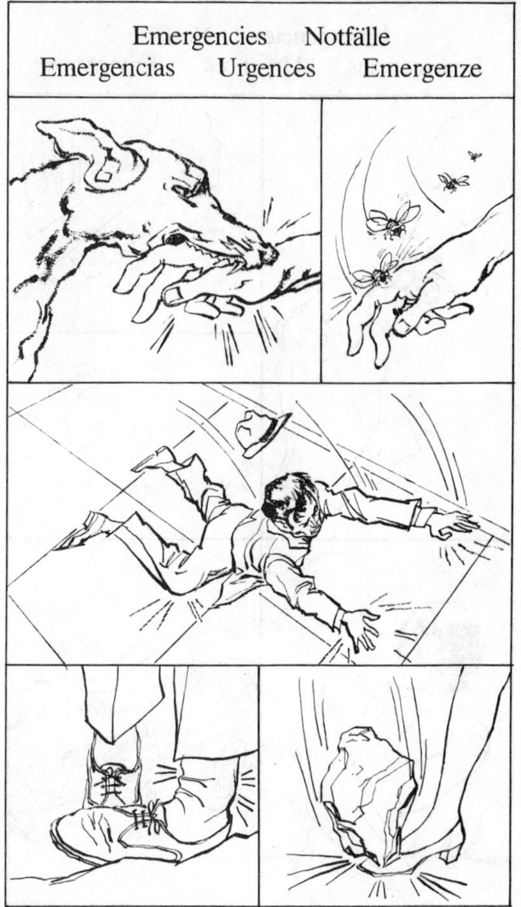
Emergencies Notfälle
Emergencias Urgences Emergenze

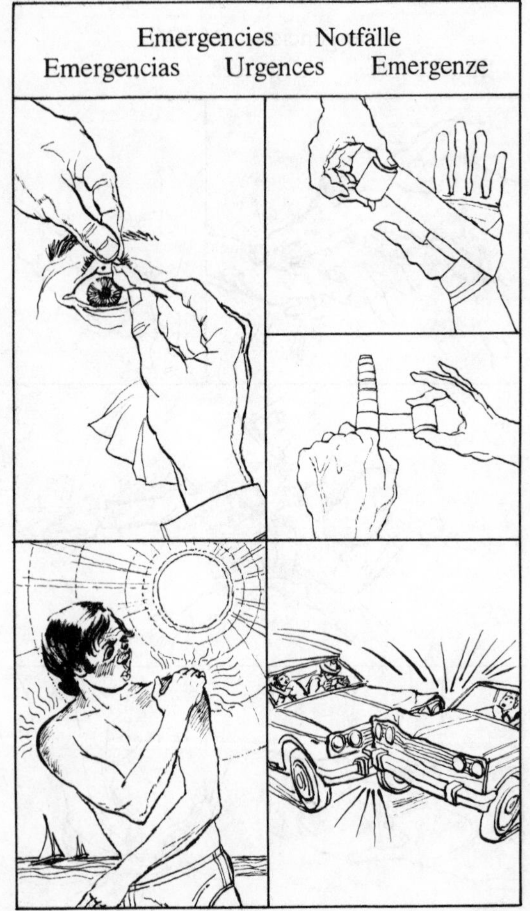
Emergencies Notfälle
Emergencias Urgences Emergenze

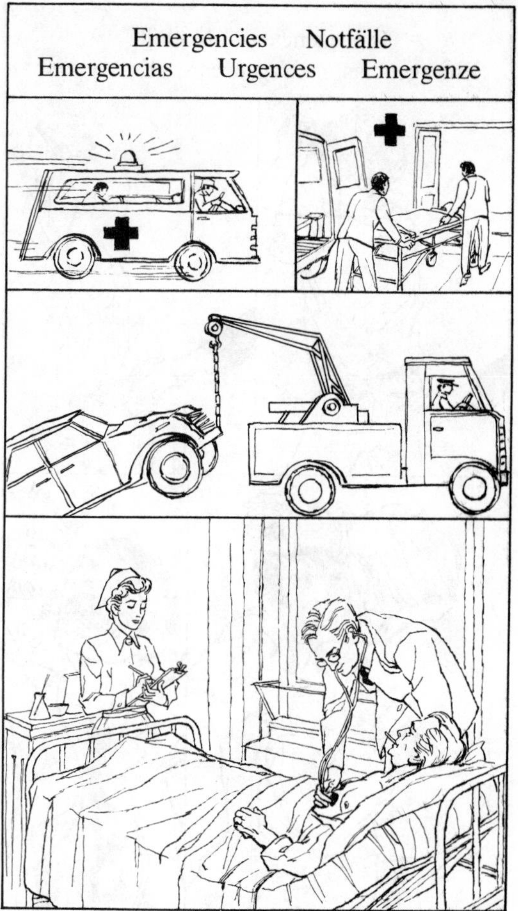
Emergencies Notfälle
Emergencias Urgences Emergenze

Emergencies Notfälle
Emergencias Urgences Emergenze

Emergencies Notfälle Emergencias Urgences Emergenze

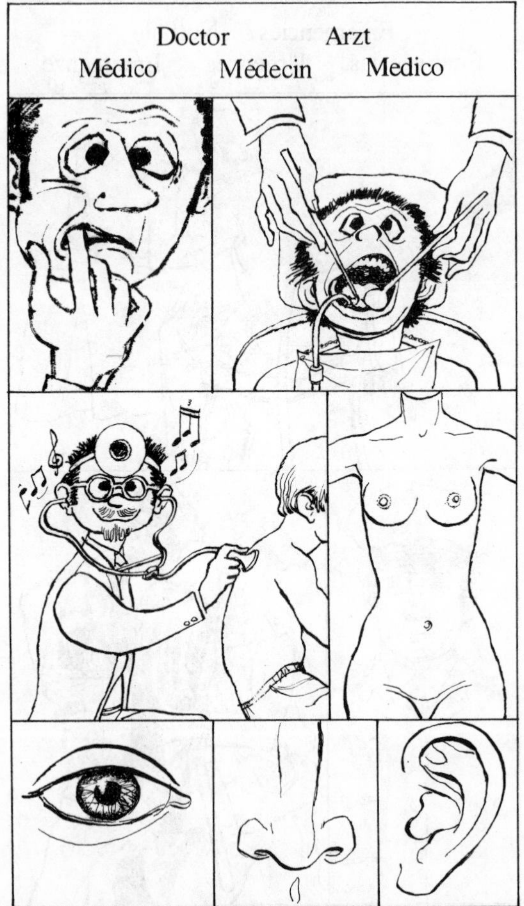
Doctor Arzt
Médico Médecin Medico

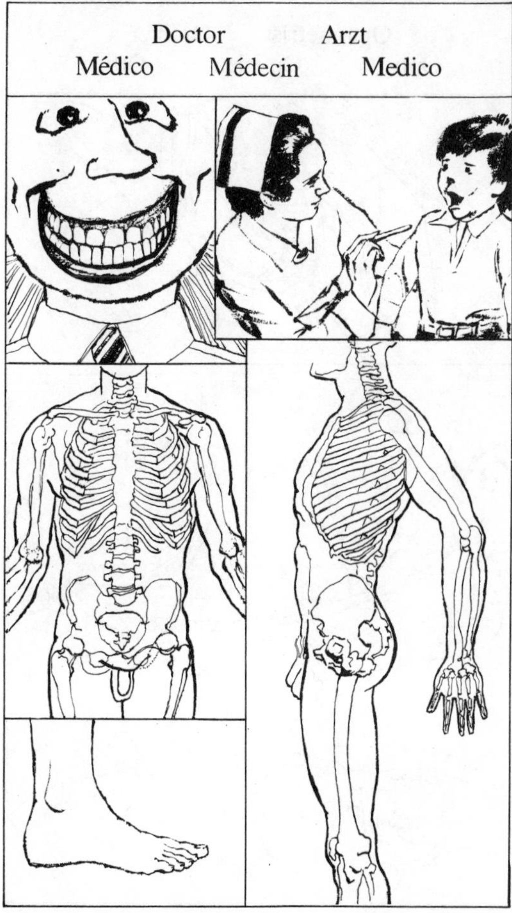
Doctor
Arzt
Médico
Médecin
Medico

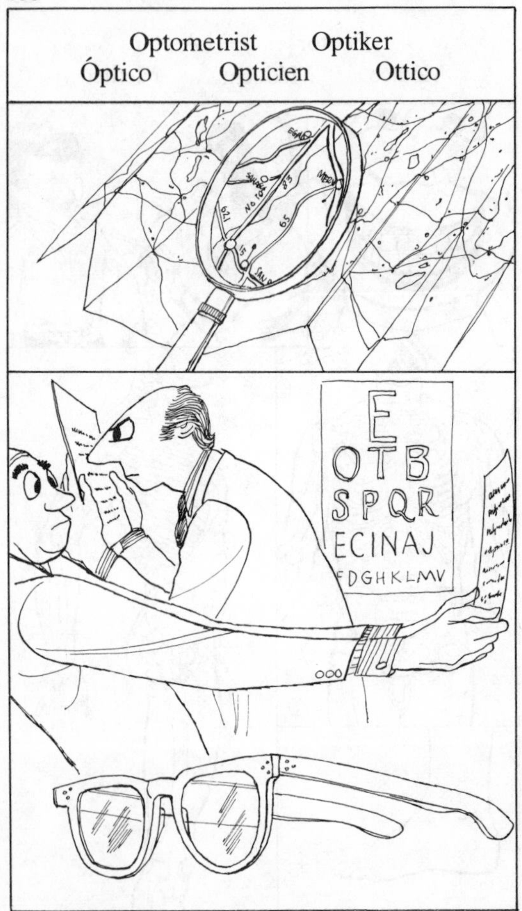
Optometrist Optiker
Óptico Opticien Ottico
E
OTB
SPQR
ECINAJ
FDGHKLMV

Optometrist Optiker
Óptico Opticien Ottico

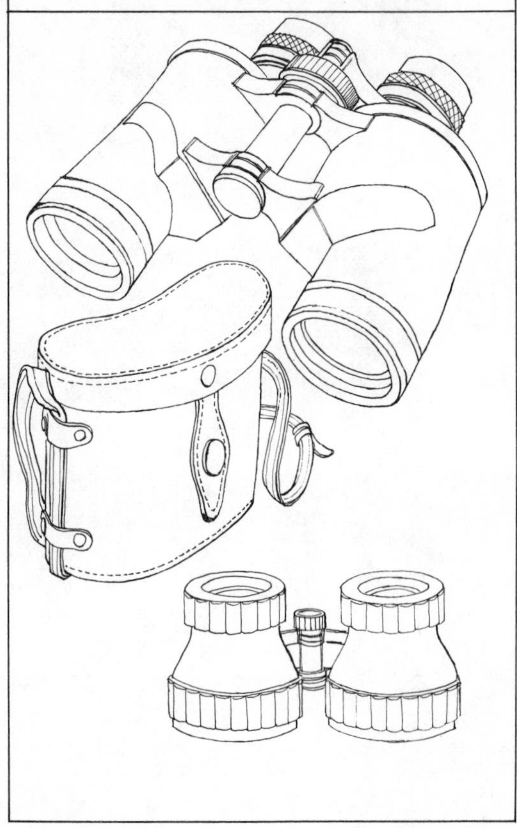

ENGLISH

Adapter plug, 4
Adhesive tape, 86
Air, 67
Air mail, 42
Airport, 54
Alarm clock, 5
Ambulance, 155
Amusements, 128–31
Animal bite, 153
Anatacid, 86
Antihistamines, 90
Apple, 26
Apricot, 29
Arch support, 91
Artichoke, 20
Ash tray, 118
Asparagus, 18
Aspirin, 86
Automobile, 66–75

Baby bottle, 91
Baby powder, 91
Back pack, 151
Bacon, 12
Badminton, 132
Baggage, 50–53
Ballet, 129
Banana, 27
Bandage, 154
Band Aid, 86
Bank, 6
Bar, 64
Baseball, 146
Basketball, 147
Bass (fish), 14
Bath mat, 3
Bath salts, 88
Bathrobe, 97, 104
Bathtub, 3
Battery (auto), 75
Beach hat, 108
Beachwear, 100, 108
Beans, 19
Beauty parlor, 38–39
Bed, 3
Beef, 11
Beer, 32
Beets, 19
Bellboy, 4
Belt, 104, 109
Beret, 107
Berth, 61
Bikes, 76–77
Bill, 31
Billiards, 137
Binding tape, 94
Binoculars, 161
Blanket, 5, 64
Blouse, 98, 109
Blowout, 68
Boiled egg, 16, 17
Bones, 159
Books, 114
Bottle (baby), 91
Bottle opener, 33
Boxer shorts, 104
Boxing, 144
Bowling, 135
Bracelets, 111
Brakes, 75
Brassiere, 96
Bread, 24
Breakfast (in room), 5
Bridge, 73
Briefs, 104, 108
Broccoli, 20
Brush (hair), 40
Bullfight, 144
Bumper, 76
Burn, 152
Bus, 80–81
Butter, 25
Buttons, 94, 95

Cabin, 61
Cable, 45, 63
Cable car, 85
Cable release (for camera), 120
Cake, 28
Calf, 10
Camera, 120–23 157
Camping, 150–51
Candelabra, 113
Candles, 150
Candy, 29
Canoe, 83
Cantaloupe, 27
Caps, 107
Carwash, 70
Cardigan, 98
Cards, 132
Carriage, 81
Carrot, 18
Casino, 130
Cauliflower, 21
Celery, 18
Chambermaid, 4
Champagne, 32
Checkers, 134
Checkroom, 52
Cheese, 25
Chef, 10
Cherries, 26
Chess, 133

Chicken, 13
China, 113
Chocolates, 29
Church, 127
Cigar, 93
Cigar holder, 93
Cigarette holder, 93
Cigarette lighter, 115
Cigarettes, 92
Circus, 129
Clamp (paper), 47
Clams, 15
Climbing, 135
Clock, 37, 111, 112
Clothes hanger, 4
Coats, 99
Coca-Cola, 33
Cocktail, 32, 33
Coffee, 30
Coffee pot, 5, 30
Collision, 154
Cologne, 40
Comb, 87
Compact, 88
Concert, 130–31
Corkscrew, 33
Cornplaster, 91
Cotton, 86
Crab, 14
Crayons, 47
Cream, 5, 30
Croissant, 24
Cruller, 28
Crystal, 117
Cucumber, 18
Cuff links, 105, 111
Cup, 30, 58
Cupcakes, 28
Currency, 6–7
Custard, 29
Cut, 152

Dancing, 130
Darts, 132
Days, 36
Deck chair, 64
Dental floss, 91
Dentist, 158–59
Deodorant, 87, 88
Desserts, 28–29
Diaper, 91
Diarrhea remedies, 91
Diary, 49
Dining car, 57
Dinner service, 113
Dirndl, 119
Doctor, 155, 158–59
Doctor's examination, 158
Dominoes, 132
Double bed, 3
Doughnut, 28
Dress, 108
Dress or suit bag, 51
Drinks, 32–33
Drugstore, 86–91
Duck, 13

Ear, 158
Earplugs, 90
Earrings, 110
Eggplant, 20
Eggs, 16–17
Electric heater, 5
Elevator, 2
Emergencies, 152–57
Enema bag, 86
Envelopes, 5, 46, 48
Eraser, 47
Evening dress, 101
Exhaust pipe, 68
Eye examination, 160
Eyebrow pencil, 88
Eyedrops, 86
Eyeglass case, 115
Eyelashes (false), 38
Eyes, 154, 158, 160
Eyeshadow, 88

Face cream, 89
Facial tissues, 86
Fall (injury), 152
Fan, 113
Fan (auto), 75
Fan (electric), 5
Fanbelt, 75
Figurines, 112
Film, 120
Filter (air), 75
Fire extinguisher, 74
First class, 58–59
Fish, 14–15
Fishing, 139
Flash gun, 123
Flashlight, 150
Flat tire, 68
Flight, 54
Foot, 159
Foot powder, 86
Football, 145
Fork, 9

Fowl, 13
Fried egg, 16
Fruit, 26–27

Garage, 2
Gargle, 90
Garlic, 20
Garter belt, 96
Gas station, 70
Gasoline, 69
Gifts, 110–19
Girdle, 96
Glass, 33
Glasses (for the eyes), 160
Glassware, 117
Gloves, 103, 104
Gondola, 82
Golf, 136
Grapes, 26
Guides, 49
Guitar, 118
Gymnasium, 62

Hairbrush, 87
Haircolor, 41
Haircoloring, 39
Haircomb, 38
Haircut, 40
Hairpins, 87
Hairset, 38
Hairspray, 39
Ham, 12
Hammer, 69
Handkerchief, 105, 116
Hardboiled egg, 17
Hatchet, 191
Hats, 100, 101, 107
Headache, 86
Heater (electric), 5
Helmet, 76
Hockey, 141
Hooks and eyes, 95
Horn, 74
Horse show, 143
Horseracing, 140
Hospital, 155
Hot water bottle, 86
Hotel, 2–5
Hunting, 138

Ice cream, 28
Ice cubes, 4
Ink, 46
Insect bite, 153
Insecticide (spray), 90
Iron, 5
Ironing board, 5

Jack, 68
Jacket, 106
Jewel box, 114
Jewelry, 110
Jigsaw puzzle, 134

Kerchief, 116
Key, 2, 52
Key case, 115
Kitchenware, 116
Knife, 9, 47, 151

Lamb, 10
Lamb, leg of, 16
Lamb chops, 10
Lantern, 130
Leather gifts, 115
Lederhosen, 119
Lemon, 26, 30, 33
Lens shade, 121
Lettuce, 18
Library, 65
Light bulb, 4
Light meter, 123
Lighter, 93, 115
Lima beans, 19
Lipstick, 88
Lobster, 15
Lollipop, 29
Lounge (plane), 55
Luggage, 50–53
Luggage carrier, 55, 74

Macaroni, 22
Magnifying glass, 49, 160
Mail, 42–45
Mailbox, 44
Manicure, 39, 41
Maps, 49
Mascara, 38
Massage (facial), 40
Mat (for a deck chair), 54
Matches, 9, 93, 160
Meat, 10–11
Mechanical pencil, 46
Melons, 27
Menu, 9
Milk, 33
Miniskirt, 99
Mirror, 76
Moccasins, 106
Months, 34–35
Monuments, 124
Motor race, 140
Motorboat, 83
Motorcycle, 76

Motorscooter, 77
Movie camera, 122
Movies, 63, 128
Muffin, 24
Muffler (car), 68
Mugging, 156
Museum, 124, 127
Mushrooms, 20

Napkins, 9, 118
Nasal spray, 90
Necklace, 110
Neckties, 105, 109
Needles, 94
Negatives (film), 123
Nightgowns, 96
Noodles, 22
Nose, 158
Notebook, 49
Nurse, 155, 159

Oil (motor), 69
Oil (salad), 31
Olive, 21
Omelet, 16
Onion, 20
Opera, 128
Opera glasses, 161
Orange, 26
Oysters, 15

Paintings, 119
Paints, 119
Pajama, 96, 104
Panties, 97
Pants, 99, 104, 108
Pantyhose, 98, 108
Paper (writing), 46
Paperclip, 47
Parfait, 29
Passport, 7
Pasta, 22–23
Paste, 49
Patient, 155
Peach, 26
Pear, 26
Pearls, 114
Peas, 18
Pedicure, 39
Pen, 46
Pencil sharpener, 47
Pencils, 46–47
Pepper, 9
Peppers (sweet), 19
Perfume, 110
Permanent (hair), 39
Pig, 12
Pillows, 5, 64
Pineapple, 27
Pins, 95
Pipes, 93
Pitcher, 117
Plate (dinner), 30
Poached egg, 17
Pole vault, 149
Police, 156, 157
Polo, 145
Porcelain, 112
Pork, 12
Porter, 50
Post, 42–45
Postage, 43
Postage stamp, 5, 43
Postman, 45
Potatoes, 22
Powder, 88
Powder puff, 88
Pullover, 98
Pumpernickel, 24
Puncture (injury), 152
Puppet theatre, 131
Purses, 114
Push-pin, 47

Rabbit, 13
Radiator (auto), 69
Radio, 118
Radio room, 118
Radishes, 19
Railroad station, 56–59
Rain boots, 109
Raincoat, 102, 107
Rain hat, 102
Raspberries, 26
Razor, 87
Razor blades, 87
Restaurant, 8–31
Ribbon, 94
Ribs of beef, 11
Rice, 22
Ring, 110, 111
Roads, 72
Roast beef, 12
Robe (bath), 97, 104
Rodeo, 142
Rolls, 5, 24
Room service, 4
Rope, 51
Rouge, 88
Rowboat, 83
Rubberband, 47
Running, 149
Rye bread, 24

Safe (hotel), 2
Safety pins, 89, 91, 95
Salad, 31
Salmon, 14
Salt, 9
Sandals, 108
Sandwich, 31
Sanitary belt, 89
Sanitary napkin, 89
Saucer, 30
Sausage, 11, 12
Scalding, 152
Scarves, 116
Scissors, 49, 95
Scrambled egg, 16
Sculpture, 112, 114, 119
Seat belt, 74
Seating, 55
Second class, 59
Service, 4
Sewing, 94–95
Shampoo (hair wash), 38
Shaver (electric), 87
Shaving brush, 87
Shaving cream, 87
Shaving stick, 87
Ships, 60–65
Shirts, 105, 108
Shock absorber, 69
Shoe brush, 5
Shoe polish, 5
Shoes, 98, 106, 108
Shoeshine, 5
Shot put, 149
Shower, 3
Shower cap, 91
Shrimp, 14
Sightseeing, 124–27
Silver service, 112
Skating, 138
Skiing, 139
Skirt, 98
Slacks, 99, 104, 108
Sleeping accommodations, 57
Sleeping bag, 151
Sleeping car, 59
Sleepware, 96, 104
Sleigh, 84
Slippers, 97, 104
Slips, 97, 108
Smoking car, 58
Smoking room, 64
Sneakers, 108
Snifter, 33
Soap, 4, 87
Soccer, 148
Socks, 105, 108
Spaghetti, 23
Spark plugs, 75
Spinach, 21
Splinter, 152
Spoon, 9
Sports, 140–49
Sprints, 149
Steering wheel, 75
Stewardess, 55, 80
Stockings, 97
Sugar, 5, 9
Soup, 31
Stamps, 42
Stateroom, 61
Stationery, 42, 46–49
Steak, 11
Stole, 101
Strap, 51
Strawberry, 26
String beans, 19
Studs (tie), 105
Subway, 79
Suit, 99, 106, 109
Sunburn, 154
Sundae, 28
Suntan lotion, 87
Superhighway, 71
Suspenders, 104
Sweaters, 102, 105
Sweets, 28–29
Swimming, 136
Swimming pool, 63
Swimsuits, 100

Table tennis, 134
Tablecloth, 118
Tables, 118
Tablespoon, 9
Tablet, 46
Tags (baggage), 48, 50
Talcum powder, 40
Tampons, 89
Tape (and dispenser), 47
Tape measure, 95
Tart, 29
Taxi, 81
Tea, 30
Teapot, 5, 30
Teaspoon, 9
Telegram, 44
Telephone, 4, 63
Television, 130
Tennis, 137
Tent, 150
Theatre, 131
Thermometer, 90

Thermos, 151
Thief, 156, 157
Thimble, 94
Thread, 94, 95
Thumb tack, 47
Tickets, 56
Tie clasp, 105
Time, 34–37
Tire chains, 68
Tires, 67
Toast, 31
Tobacco, 92–93
Toilet, 3, 58, 63, 90
Toilet paper 3, 90
Tomato, 18
Toothache, 198
Toothbrush, 87
Toothpaste, 87
Tow-truck, 155
Towel, 4
Track, 148–49
Traffic lights, 73
Train, 56–59
Transparencies, 123
Transportation, 54–59
Traveler's check, 6
Tripod, 122
Trivet, 117
Trout, 14
Trunk, 53
T-shirt, 108
Tunnel, 71
Turkey, 13
Turnips, 19
Tuxedo, 107
Tweezers, 38
Twin beds, 3
Twine, 48
Twisted ankle, 153

Umbrellas, 102–4
Undershirt, 104, 108
Underwear, 104, 108
Upset stomach, 86

Vacuum bottle, 151
Vase, 119
Veal, 10
Vegetables, 18–21
Vest, 106
Vinegar, 31
Voltages, 4

Wallet, 115, 156
Washroom, 58
Water, 33, 69
Watermelon, 27
Windshield, 77
Wine, 32
Wrenches, 69
Wrestling, 146
Wrist watch, 111
Writing paper, 5, 46
Writing room, 65

Zipper, 104

DEUTSCH

Abendkleidung, 101
Ambulanz, 155
Ananas, 27
Angreifung, 156
Antihistamin, 90
Anzug, 99, 106, 109
Apfel, 26
Apfelsine, 26
Apotheke, 86–91
Aprikose, 29
Armbände, 111
Armbanduhr, 111
Artischocke, 20
Arzt, 155, 158–59
Ärztliche Untersuchung, 158
Aschenbecher, 118
Aspirin, 86
Aufzug, 2
Augen, 154, 158, 160
Augenbrauenstift, 88
Augenschatten, 88
Augenschminke, 38
Augentropfen, 86
Augenuntersuchung, 160
Auspuffrohr, 68
Austern, 15
Autobahn, 71
Autobus, 80, 81
Automobilwäscherei, 70
Bad, 3
Badeanzüge, 100
Badehaube, 91
Badematte, 3
Badesalze, 88
Badezimmer, 58
Bahnhof, 56–59
Ballett, 129
Banane, 27
Band, 94
Bandmass, 95
Bank, 6
Bar, 64
Baseball, 146
Baskenmütze, 104, 109
Basketball, 147
Batterie, 75
Baumwolle, 86
Beefsteak, 11
Beförderung, 54–59
Benzin, 69
Bergsteigen, 133
Besteck, 113
Bett, 3
Bettdecke, 5, 64
Bibliothek, 65
Bier, 32
Bildhauerkunst, 112, 114, 119
Billardspiel, 137
Bindegürtel, 89
Birne, 26
Bisswunde, 153
Bleistifte, 47
Bleistiftspitzer, 47
Blitzlampe, 123
Blumenkohl, 21
Bluse, 98, 109
Bohnen, 19
Boxen, 144
Brandwunde, 152
Brausebad, 3
Briefkasten, 44
Briefmarke, 5, 43
Briefmarken, 42
Brieftasche (verlust von der), 156
Briefträger, 45
Briefumschläge, 46
Brillen, 160
Brillenetui, 115
Broccoli, 20
Brot, 24
Brücke, 173
Bücher, 114
Bügelbrett, 5
Bürste, 40
Büstenhalter, 96
Butter, 25

Camping, 150–51
Coca-Cola, 33
Cocktail, 32, 33
Cognac (ein Gläschen), 33

Damenbinden, 89
Damenschlüpfer, 97
Damespiel, 134
Dauerwelle, 39
Denkmäler, 124
Desodorierungsmittel, 87, 88
Diapositiven, 123
Dieb, 156, 157
Dirndl, 119
Dominospiel, 132
Doppelbett, 3
Doppelbetten, 3

Drahtauslöser, 120
Dreifuss, 117
Druckbilder, 119
Durchfallmedezin, 91

Eier, 16–17
Eiscreme, 29
Eierpflanze, 20
Eisstücke, 4
Elektrischer Heizkörper, 5
Elektrischer Rasierapparat, 87
Ente, 13
Erbsen, 18
Erdbeeren, 26
Erste Klasse, 59
Essig, 31
Esslöffel, 9

Fächer, 113
Faden, 94, 95
Fahrkarten, 56
Fahrrad, 77–78
Fall, 152
Feder, 46
Feldstecher, 161
Fernseher, 130
Fernsprecher, 4, 63
Feuerlöschapparat, 74
Feuerzeug, 93, 115
Figuren, 112
Film, 120
Filmkamera, 122
Fingerhut, 94
Fisch, 14–15
Fischen, 139
Flaschenöffner, 33
Fleisch, 10–11
Flug, 54
Flughafen, 54
Flugpost, 42
Forelle, 14
Früchte, 26–27
Fruchteiscreme, 28
Frühstück, 5
Fuss, 159
Fussball, 145
Fussballspiel, 148
Fusspflege, 39
Fusspuder, 86

Gabel, 9
Garage, 2
Garderobe, 52
Garnele, 14
Geflügel, 13
Gegenlichtblende, 121
Geldschrank, 2
Geldtasche, 115
Gemälde, 119
Gemüse, 18–21
Gepäck, 50–53
Gepäckmarken, 48, 50
Gepäcksraum, 50
Gepäckträger, 51, 55, 74
Geröstetes Brot, 31
Geschenke, 110–119
Gesichtsmassage, 40
Gesichtssalbe, 89
Gestrickte Wollweste, 98
Getränke, 32–33
Gitarre, 118
Glace, 28
Glas, 33
Glaswaren, 117
Glühbirne, 4
Golfspiel, 136
Gondel, 82
Grüne Bohnen, 19
Gummibändchen, 47
Gurgelwasser, 90
Gurke, 18
Gürtel, 75, 104, 109

Haarbürste, 87
Haarfärbemittel, 41
Haarfärbung, 39
Haarlack, 89
Haarnadeln, 87
Haarschnitt, 38, 40
Haarwaschen, 38
Haken und Ösen, 95
Halsband, 110
Halstücher, 116
Hammer, 69
Handbeil, 191
Handschuhe, 103, 104
Handtuch, 4
Hartes Ei, 17
Hauptkoch, 10
Hautöl, 87
Hebewinde, 68
Heftband, 47
Heftnagel, 47
Heizkörper, 69
Helm, 77
Hemde, 105, 108
Himbeeren, 26

Hockey, 141
Hörnchen, 24
Hosen, 99, 104, 108
Hosenstrümpfe, 98, 108
Hosenträger, 104
Hotel, 2–5
Hotelpage, 4
Hühnchen, 13
Hühneraugenpflaster, 91
Hundehütte, 62, 63
Hummer, 15
Hupe, 74
Hüte, 100, 101, 107

Insektenpulver, 90

Jacke, 106
Jagen, 138
Jigsawrätsel, 134

Kabeldepesche, 45, 63
Kabine, 61
Kaffee, 30
Kaffeetopf, 5, 30
Kalb, 10
Kalbfleisch, 10
Kamera, 120–23, 157
Kamm, 87
Kandelaber, 113
Kaninchen, 13
Kanoe, 83
Karrotte, 18
Kartoffeln, 22
Käse, 25
Kegeln, 135
Kerzen, 150
Kinderpuder, 91
Kino, 63, 128
Kirche, 127
Kirschen, 26
Klammer für Papier, 47
Kleid, 108
Kleidhänger, 4
Kleine Kuchen, 28
Kleister, 49
Klistierspritze, 86
Klosettpapier, 3, 90
Knoblauch, 20
Knochen, 159
Knöpfe, 94, 95
Koffer, 51, 53
Kölnisches Wasser, 40
Konzert, 130–31
Kopfkissen, 5, 64
Kopfsalat, 18
Kopfschmerzen, 86
Kopftuch, 116
Korkzieher, 33
Korsett, 96
Krabbe, 14
Kragenknopf, 105
Krankenhaus, 155
Krankenschwester, 155, 159
Krapfen, 28
Kravaten, 105, 109
Kravatenklippe, 105
Kringel, 28
Krug, 117
Küchegeschirr, 116
Kuchen, 28
Kugelstossen, 149
Kühltrank, 132
Kunstdruckbilder, 119
Künstliche Augenwimpern, 38
Kunstreiterei, 143
Kurs, 6–7

Lachs, 14
Lammfleisch, 10
Lammkeule, 16
Lammkoteletts, 10
Landkarten, 49
Lanterne, 130
Lauf, 149
Lederhosen, 119
Lederstreifen, 51
Lederwaren, 115
Leukoplast, 86, 94
Lichtmesser, 123
Liegestuhl, 64
Limabohnen, 19
Lippenstift, 88
Löffel, 9
Luft, 67
Lüfter, 5, 75
Luftfilter, 75
Luxuskabine, 61

Makkaroni, 22
Maniküre, 39, 41
Manschettenknöpfe, 105, 111
Mäntel, 99
Matte, 54
Meeresmuschel, 15
Melanzani, 20
Melonen, 27
Messer, 9, 47, 151
Mieder, 96

Milch, 33
Minirock, 99
Mohrrübe, 18
Mokassiner, 106
Monate, 34–35
Morgenrock, 97, 104
Motorboot, 83
Motorrad, 76
Motorroller, 77
Museum, 124, 127
Mützen, 107

Nachthemde, 96, 104
Nachtisch, 28–29
Nadeln, 94
Nähen, 94–95
Nase, 158
Nasespritzung, 90
Negativen, 123
Notfäilen, 152–57
Notizbuch, 49
Nudeln, 22

Ohr, 158
Ohrringe, 110
Ohrstopfel, 90
Öl, 69
Olive, 21
Olivenöl, 31
Omelette, 16
Oper, 128
Operngläser, 161

Pantoffeln, 97, 104
Papier, 46
Papierklammer, 47
Paprikaschoten, 19
Parfüm, 110
Pastellstifte, 47
Patient, 155
Perlen, 114
Pelzkragen, 101
Pfeffer, 9
Pfeifen, 93
Pferderennen, 140
Pfirsich, 26
Pflaster, 86
Pilze, 20
Pinzette, 38
Polizei, 156, 157
Polo, 145
Porto, 43
Porzellan, 112, 113
Post, 42–45
Puder, 88
Puderdose, 88
Puderquaste, 88
Pullover, 98
Pumpernickel, 24
Punktur, 152
Puppenspiel, 131
Push-pin, 47

Radiergummi, 47
Rahm, 5, 30
Rasiercreme, 87
Rasierklingen, 87
Rasiermesser, 87
Rasierpinsel, 87
Rasierriemen, 87
Raucher, 58
Rauchzimmer, 64
Rechnung, 31
Regenhut, 102
Regenmantel, 102, 107
Regenschirme, 102–4
Regenstiefel, 109
Reifen, 67
Reifenpanne, 68
Reis, 22
Reiseleiter, 49
Reisepass, 7
Reisescheck, 6
Reissverschluss, 104
Restaurant, 8–9, 30–31
Rettiche, 19
Rinderbraten, 12
Rindfleisch, 11
Rindsrippenstück, 11
Ring, 110, 111
Ringen, 146
Rock, 98
Roggenbrot, 24
Rüben, 19
Rüben, weisse, 19
Rucksack, 151
Ruderboot, 83
Ruderleibchen, 108
Rühreier, 16
Rundfunk, 118
Rundfunkgramm, 63

Sahne, 5, 30
Salat, 31
Salon, 55
Salz, 9
Sandalen, 108
Sandwich, 31
Saugflasche, 91
Schach, 134
Schal, 116
Schalldämpfer, 68
Schere, 49, 95
Schiffe, 60–65
Schinken, 12

Schlafanzug, 96, 104
Schlafgelegenheiten, 57
Schlafkoje, 61
Schlafsachen, 96, 104
Schlafsack, 151
Schleppwagen, 155
Schlitten, 84
Schlittschuhlaufen, 138
Schlüssel, 52
Schlüsseletui, 115
Schlüsseln, 2
Schminke, 88
Schmuck, 110
Schmuckschrank, 114
Schneeketten, 68
Schneeschuhlaufen, 139
Schnittwunde, 152
Schokoladen, 29
Schönheitssalon, 38–39
Schraubbleistift, 46
Schraubenschlüsseln, 69
Schreibpapier, 5, 46
Schreibtafel, 46
Schreibwaren, 42, 46–49
Schreibzimmer, 65
Schuhbürste, 5
Schuhcreme, 5
Schuhe, 98, 106, 108
Schuheinsatz, 91
Schwein, 12
Schweinefleisch, 12
Schwimmbad, 63
Schwimmen, 136
Seebarsch, 14
Segeltuchschuhe, 108
Sehenswürdigkeiten, 124–27
Seidenpapier, 86
Seife, 4, 87
Seil, 51
Seilbahn, 85
Sekt, 32
Sellerie, 18
Semeln, 5, 24
Semmelkuchen, 24
Serviette, 9, 118
Shuhcreme, 5
Shuhputzen, 5
Sicherheitsgürteln, 74
Sicherheitsnadeln, 89, 91, 95
Silberwaren, 112
Sitzplan, 55
Smoking, 107
Socken, 105, 108
Sonnenbrand, 154
Spaghetti, 23
Spannungen, elektromotorische, 4
Spargel, 18
Speck, 12
Speisekarte, 9
Speisewagen, 57
Spiegel, 77
Spiegeleie, 16
Spiegelreflexkamera, 121
Spielbank, 130
Spielkarten, 132
Spinat, 21
Splitter, 152
Sport, 140–49
Sporthosen, 99, 104, 108
Stabhochsprung, 149
Stativ, 122
Stecknadeln, 95
Steuerrad, 75
Stewardess, 55, 80
Stich, 153
Stiefel, 99, 102, 106, 109
Stierkampf, 144
Stossdämpfer, 69
Stosstange, 77
Strahlungsheizung, 5
Strandhut, 108
Strandkleidung, 100, 108
Strassen, 72
Streichhölzer, 9, 93, 160
Strick, 48
Strumpf, 97
Strumpfbandgürtel, 96
Stuhl, 112
Suppe, 31
Süssigkeiten, 28, 29

Tabak, 92–93
Tage, 36
Tagebuch, 49
Talk, 40
Tampone, 89
Tankstelle, 70

Tanz, 130
Taschen, 114
Taschenlampe, 150
Taschentuch, 105, 116
Tasse, 30, 58
Taxi, 81
Tee, 30
Teekanne, 5, 30
Teelöffel, 9
Teigwaren, 22–23
Telegramm, 44
Teller, 30
Tennis, 137
Theater, 131
Thermometer, 90
Thermosflasche, 151
Tinte, 46
Tische, 118
Tischtennis, 133
Tischtuch, 118
Toilette, 18
Tomate, 18
Torte, 29
Transformator, 4
Truthahn, 13
Tunnel, 71
Turnhalle, 62

Überzieher, 99
Uhr, 37, 111, 112
Unterbeinkleider, 104, 108
Untergrundbahn, 79
Unterhaltungen, 128–31
Unterhemd, 104, 108
Unterhosen, 104, 108
Unterröcke, 97, 108
Untertasse, 30
Unterwäsche, 104, 108

Vase, 119
Ventilator, 75
Ventilatorriemen, 75
Verband, 154
Vergrösserungsglas, 49, 160
Verkehrsampeln, 73
Verklärter Magen, 86
Verlorenes Ei, 17
Verstauchung, 153

Wagen, 66–75, 81
Warmeflasche, 86
Warzenmelone, 27
Wasser, 33, 69
Wassermelone, 27
Weckuhr, 5
Weichës, Ei, 16
Wein, 32
Weintrauben, 26
Weste, 106
Wettfahrt, 140
Wildwestvorführung, 142
Windel, 91
Windschutzscheibe, 77
Wollweste, 102, 105
Wurfspiesser, 132
Wurst, 11, 12

Zahnarzt, 158–59
Zahnbürste, 87
Zahnpaste, 87
Zahnschmerzen, 198
Zahnzwirn, 91
Zeit, 34–37
Zelt, 150
Zigaretten, 92
Zigarettenspitze, 93
Zigarre, 93
Zigarrenspitze, 93
Zimmerbedienung, 4
Zimmermädchen, 4
Zirkus, 129
Zitrone, 26, 30, 33
Zucker, 5, 9
Zuckerwerk, 29
Zug, 56–59
Zündkerzen, 75
Zusammensatzspiel, 134
Zusstoss, 154
Zweite Klasse, 59
Zwiebel, 20

ESPAÑOL

Abanico, 113
Abre-bottelas, 33
Abrigos, 99
Aceite, 69
Aceituna, 21
Aeropuerto, 54
Afilalápices, 47
Agua, 33, 69
Agujas, 94
Aire, 67
Ajedrez, 133
Ajo, 20
Alcachofa, 20
Aldaricoque, 29
Aldornoz, 98
Alfiler, 95
Alfiler de corbata, 105
Algodón, 86
Almejas, 15
Almohados, 5, 64
Ambulancia, 155
Amortiguador, 69
Ananás, 27
Anteojos, 160
Antiacido, 86
Antihistamina, 86
Apio, 18
Arco suporte, 91
Aretes, 110
Arroz, 22
Asalto, 156
Ascensor, 2
Aspirina, 86
Astilla, 152
Autobús, 80, 81
Automóvil, 66–75
Ave, 13
Azúcar, 5–9
Badminton, 132
Baile, 130
Ballet, 129
Banco, 6
Baño, 3
Bar, 64
Barcós, 60–65
Basquetbol, 147
Batas, 97, 104
Bateria, 75
Baúl, 53
Bebidas, 32, 33
Baseball, 146
Berenjema, 20
Betún, 5
Biberón, 91
Biblioteca, 65
Bicicleta, 77–78
Biftec, 11
Billar, 137
Billetes, 56
Bloc, 46
Blusa, 98, 109
Bocina, 74
Boina, 107
Bolos (juego de), 133
Bolsa de agua caliente, 86
Bolsas, 114
Bombonés, 4, 29
Boquilla, 93
Borla, 88
Botas, 99, 102, 106, 109
Botas de lluvia, 109
Bote, 83
Botónes, 94, 95
Boxeo, 144
Broche, 95
Broche de afeitar, 87
Bróculi, 20
Bruselas, 38
Bujia, 75
Buzón, 44

Cablegrama, 45, 63
Cadenas de llanta, 68
Café, 30
Cafetera, 5, 30
Caja de caudales, 2
Caida, 152
Calcetines, 105, 108
Calentador eléctrico, 5
Calzoncillos, 104, 108
Cama, 3
Cama di matrimonio, 3
Cámara cinematografica, 122
Cámaras, 120–23, 157
Camarera, 4
Camarote, 61
Camas gemelas, 3
Camerera, 55, 80
Camerón, 14
Camerote, 61
Camino, 72
Camiseta, 104, 108
Camisas, 105, 108
Camisola, 108
Candelas, 150
Cangrejo, 14
Canoa, 83

Canoa automóvil, 83
Cantalupo, 27
Carne, 10–11
Carne de cerdo, 12
Carne de res, 11
Carrera de carro, 140
Carreras de caballos, 140
Carretera, 71
Cartas, 132
Cartera, 115
Cartero, 45
Casco, 77
Casino, 130
Caza, 138
Cebolla, 20
Cenicero, 118
Cepillo, 40
Cepillo de cabeza, 87
Cepillo de dientes, 87
Cepillo de zapato, 5
Cerezas, 26
Cerveza, 32
Chaleco, 106
Chalinas, 116
Champaña, 32
Champú, 38
Chaqueta, 106
Cheque de viajeros, 6
Chiles dulces, 19
China, 113
Chinche, 47
Chocolates, 29
Chuletas de cordero, 10
Cigarrillos, 92
Cine, 63, 128
Cinta, 94
Cinta metrica, 95
Cinturón, 104, 109
Cinturóne de asiento, 74
Circo, 129
Clip, 47
Coca-Cola, 33
Coche, 81
Coche comedor, 57
Coche fumador, 58
Coctel, 32–33
Colgadores (de ropa), 4
Coliflor, 21
Colisión, 154
Collar, 110
Colorete, 88
Colonia, 40
Combinación, 97, 108
Concierto, 130–31
Concurso hipico, 143
Conejo, 13
Copa grande para coñac, 33
Corbatas, 105, 109
Cordero, 10
Correa, 51
Correo, 42–45
Correo aéreo, 42
Corrida de toros, 144
Corsé, 96
Corte de pelo, 40
Costillas de res, 11
Costura, 94–95
Crema de afeitar, 87
Crema de belleza, 89
Crema de sol, 87
Crema para los párpados, 88
Cremallera, 104
Cristalería, 117
Cuaderno, 49
Cuarto de escribir, 65
Cuarto de radio, 63
Cubito de hielo, 4
Cuchara, 9
Cuchera de sopa, 9
Cucharita, 9
Cuchillado, 152
Cuchillo, 9, 47, 151
Cuenta, 31
Cuerda, 51
Cuernitos, 24
Cuero, 115
Curita, 86

Damas, 135
Dedal, 94
Dentista, 158–59
Deportes, 140–49
Desayuno, 5
Desodorante, 87, 88
Despertador, 5
Destral, 191
Diario, 49
Diarrea (remedios), 91
Días, 36
Dirndl, 119
Diversiones, 128–31

Dolor de cabeza, 86
Dolor de dientes, 198
Dominó, 132
Ducha, 3
Dulces, 28–29
Durasno, 26

Embalaje, 149
Emergencias, 152–57
Emparedado, 31
Emplasto (para los callos), 91
Encendedor, 93, 115
Enfermera, 155, 159
Engrudo, 49
Ensalada, 31
Equipaje, 50–53
Escala tipográfica ofalmométrica, 160
Escaldadura, 152
Escultura, 112, 114, 119
Espárrago, 18
Espejo, 77
Espinacas, 21
Esquiismo, 139
Estación de ferrocarriles, 56–59
Estampillas, 42
Estera, 54
Estola, 101
Estuche de afeites, 88
Estuche de lentes, 115
Etiquetas, 48, 50
Excusado, 3, 58, 63
Exposimetro, 123
Extintor, 74

Falda, 98
Farmacia, 86–91
Favas, 19
Figurillas, 112
Fijapeinados, 38
Filtro de air, 75
Flan, 29
Florero, 119
Fósforos, 9, 93, 160
Frambuesas, 26
Franqueo, 43
Frazada, 5, 64
Frenos, 75
Fresas, 26
Fruta, 26–27
Fumadero, 64
Función de titeres, 131
Fútbol, 145

Gafas, 160
Garage, 2
Gargarismo, 90
Gasolina, 69
Gato, 68
Gemelos, 105, 111, 161
Gemlos de teatro, 161
Gimnasio, 62
Golf, 136
Goma de borrar, 47
Góndola, 82
Gorro de baño, 91
Gotas, 90
Gotas para las ojas, 86
Guantes, 103, 104
Guarda joyas, 114
Guardarropa, 52
Guias, 49
Guisantes, 18
Guita, 48
Guitarra, 118

Habichuelas, 19
Habitación, 57
Helado, 28
Helado con frutas, 28
Hilo, 94, 95
Hockey, 141
Hojitas de afeitar, 87
Hongos, 20
Horquillas, 87
Hospital, 115
Hotel, 2–5
Huesos, 159
Huevo duro, 17
Huevo escalfado, 17
Huevo frito, 16
Huevo pasado por agua, 16
Huevos, 16–17
Huevos revueltos, 16

Iglesia, 127
Imperdible, 89, 91, 95
Impermeable, 102, 107

Indisposición, 86
Insecticida, 90

Jabon, 4, 87
Jamón, 12
Jarro, 117
Jefe de cocina, 10
Joyas, 110
Judias verdes, 19

Kleenex, 86

Laca de pelo, 89
Ladrón, 156, 157
Lampára relampago, 123
Langosta, 15
Lápiz, 46, 47
Lápiz labial, 88
Lápiz para las cejas, 88
Lavabo, 58
Lavativa, 86
Leche, 33
Lechuga, 18
Lederhosen, 119
Legumbres, 18–21
Libros, 114
Liga de goma, 47
Liquero, 96
Limón, 26, 30, 33
Linterna, 130, 150
Lista de platos, 9
Llanta desinflada, 68
Llantas, 67
Llave, 2
Llave inglesa, 69
Llavero, 115
Llaves, 52
Lucha, 146
Lupa, 49, 160
Lustre, 5
Luz de tráfico, 73

Macarrones, 22
Manicura, 39, 41
Manteca, 25
Mantel, 118
Mantequilla, 25
Manzana, 26
Mapas, 49
Máquina de afeitar, 87
Martillo, 69
Masaje, 40
Medias, 97
Médico, 155, 158–59
Melocotón, 26
Melónes, 27
Mesas, 34–35
Metro, 79
Minifalda, 99
Mocasines, 106
Mollete, 24
Moneda, 6–7
Monumentos, 124
Motoneta, 77
Motorcicleta, 76
Mozo, 50
Museo, 124, 127

Nabos, 19
Naranja, 26
Nariz, 158
Nata, 5, 30
Natación, 136
Navaja de afeitar, 87

Oído, 158
Ojos, 154, 158, 160
Olio, 31
Ópera, 128
Oreja, 158
Ostras, 15

Paciente, 155
Paleta, 29
Pan, 24
Pan tostado, 31
Pañal, 91
Pancake, 28
Pando centeno, 24
Panecillos, 5, 24
Pantalones, 99, 104, 108
Pantimedias, 98, 108
Pañuelo, 105, 116
Papas, 22
Papel, 46
Papel agesivo, 47
Papel de escribir, 5, 46
Papel higiénico, 3, 90
Papel para cartas, 42, 46–49
Parabrisas, 77
Parachoques, 77
Paraguas, 102–4
Parfait, 29
Passport, 7
Pasta, 22–23
Pasta dentifrica, 87
Patinaje, 138
Pato, 13
Pavo, 13
Pedicure, 39
Peinado, 38
Peine, 87
Pelicula, 120

Pepino, 18
Pera, 26
Perfume, 110
Perlas, 114
Permanente, 39
Perrera, 62, 63
Pesca, 139
Pescado, 14–15
Pestañas falsas, 38
Picadura, 153
Pie, 159
Pierna de oveja, 16
Pijama, 96, 104
Pimienta, 9
Pinturas, 119
Pipas, 93
Piscina, 63
Plancha, 5
Plátano, 27
Platillo, 30
Plato, 30
Pluma, 46
Policia, 156, 157
Pollo, 13
Polo, 145
Polvo para los pies, 86
Polvo para nenes, 91
Polvos, 88
Polvos de talco, 40
Porcelana, 112
Postres, 28–29
Primera clase, 58, 59
Prueba negativa, 123
Puente, 73
Puerco, 12
Puesto de gasolina, 70
Pulseras, 111
Pumpernickel, 24
Puntura, 152
Puro, 93

Quemado por el sol, 154
Quemadura, 152
Queso, 25

Rábanos, 19
Radiador, 69
Radio, 118
Regalos, 110–19
Rehiletes, 132
Reloj, 37, 111, 112
Reloj de pulsera, 111
Remolachas, 19
Remolcador, 155
Restaurante, 8–9, 30–31
Ribete, 94
Róbalo, 14
Rodeo, 142
Rompecabezas, 134
Ropa interior, 104, 108
Rosbif, 12
Rosquilla, 28

Saco, 51
Saco de dormir, 151
Sal, 9
Sal de baño, 88
Salchicha, 11, 12
Salón de belleza, 38–39
Salón social, 55
Salmón, 14
Salto con garrocha, 149
Sandalias, 108
Sandia, 27
Secunda clase, 59
Sientas, 55
Sello, 5, 43
Servicio, 4
Servilleta, 9, 118
Silenciador, 68
Silla, 112
Silla de cubierta, 64
Smoking, 107
Sobres, 5, 46, 48
Sombrero de lluvia, 109
Sombrero de playa, 108
Sombreros, 100, 101, 107
Sopa, 31
Sortija, 110, 111
Sostén, 96
Spaghetti, 23
Subida, 135
Suéteres, 102, 105
Sujetapapeles, 47
Sweater, 98

Tabaco, 92–93
Tabala de planchar, 15
Tafetán adhesivo, 86
Tafete de baño, 3
Tafón de oidos, 90
Tallarines, 22
Tarta, 29
Taxi, 81

Taza, 30, 58
Té, 30
Teatro, 131
Teléfono, 4, 63
Telegrama, 44
Televisión, 130
Tenedor, 9
Tenis, 137
Tenis de mesa, 133
Termómetro, 90
Termos, 151
Ternera, 10
Tetera, 5, 30
Tiempo, 34–37
Tienda, 150
Tijeras, 49, 95
Tinta, 46
Tinte para el pelo, 41
Tinte para las pestañas, 38
Tirabuzón, 33
Tirantes, 104
Tiro de la pesa, 149
Toalla, 4
Toallas higiénica, 89
Tobilla torsido, 153
Tocino, 12
Tomate, 18
Torta, 28
Tortilla de huevos, 16
Traje, 99, 106, 109
Traje de baño, 100
Traje de dormir, 96, 104
Traje de noche, 101
Trajes de playa, 100, 108
Transformador, 4
Transparencias, 123
Transportación, 54–59
Tranvía (por cable), 85
Trebedes, 117
Tren, 56–59
Trineo, 84
Tripod, 122
Trucha, 14
Tubo de escape, 68
Túnel, 71

Utensilios de cacina, 116
Uva, 26

Vajilla, 113
Vajilla de plata, 112
Vendaje, 154
Vestido, 108
Vinagre, 31
Vino, 32
Visita de puntos de interés, 124–27
Visita médica, 158
Volante, 75
Voltaje, 4
Vaso, 33
Vuelo, 54

Zanahoria, 18
Zapatillas, 97, 104
Zapatos, 98, 106, 108
Zapatos blandos, 108
Zurrón, 156

FRANÇAIS

Abricot, 29
Addition, 31
Aéroport, 54
Affranchissement, 43
Agenda, 49
Agneau, 10
Agrafe, 47
Agrafe et oeillet, 43
Aiguilles, 94
Ail, 20
Allocation des sièges, 55
Allumettes, 9, 93, 160
Alpinisme, 135
Ambulance, 155
Amortisseur, 69
Ampoule, 4
Ananas, 27
Antiacide, 86
Antihistamines, 90
Appareil reflex, 121
Appareils photographiques, 120–23, 157
Argenterie, 112
Artichaut, 20
Ascenseur, 2
Asperges, 18
Aspirine, 86
Assiette, 30
Aubergine, 20
Auto, 66–75
Autobus, 80, 81
Autocar, 80, 81
Autoroute, 71
Bagages, 50–53
Bague, 110, 111
Bain, 3
Ballet, 129
Banane, 27
Bandage, 154
Bande de papier gommé, 47
Banque, 6
Bar, 64
Bas, 97
Baseball, 146
Basketball, 147
Bateau à rames, 83
Bâton de savon pour la barbé, 87
Batterie, boîte à accu, 75
Batterie de cuisine, 116
Beignet, 28
Beret, 107
Betteraves, 19
Beurre, 25
Biberon, 91
Bibliotèque, 65
Bière, 32
Bifteck, 11
Bijou, 110
Billard, 137
Billets, 56
Blaireau, 87
Blouse, 98, 109
Boeuf, 11
Boissons, 32–33
Boîte aux lettres, 44
Bonbons, 28, 29
Bonnet de bain, 91
Bonnets, 107
Bottes, 99, 102, 106, 109
Boucles d'oreille, 110
Bougies, 75, 150
Bouillotte, 86
Boules quies, 90
Bouteille thermos, 151
Boutons, 94, 95
Boutons jumelés, 105, 111
Bowling, 133
Boxe, 144
Bracelets, 111
Bretelles, 104
Briquet, 115
Brocoli, 20
Brosse à chaussures, 5
Brosse à cheveux, 40, 87
Brosse à dents, 87
Brûlure, 152

Cabine, 61
Cabinet de toilette, 58
Cablogramme, 45, 63
Cadeaux, 110–19
Café, 30
Cafetière, 5, 30
Caleçon, 104
Camera, 122
Camping, 150–51
Canard, 13
Candélabre, 113
Caoutchouc, 109
Canoë, 83

Canot automobile, 83
Cantaloup, 27
Carnet, 49
Carotte, 18
Cartes géographiques, 49
Cartes (jeu de), 132
Casino, 130
Casque, 76
Ceinture, 104, 109
Ceinture de sécurité, 74
Ceinture périodique, 89
Céleri, 18
Cendrier, 118
Cerises, 26
Cervette, 14
Chaînes, 68
Cheville foulé, 153
Chiase, 112
Chaise longue de bord, 64
Chambre à deux lits, 3
Champagne, 32
Champignons, 20
Chandails, 98, 102, 105
Chandelles, 150
Chapeau de plage, 108
Chapeau de pluie, 102
Chapeaux, 100, 101, 107
Chasse, 138
Chausettes, 105, 108
Chaussures, 98, 106, 108
Chèque de voyageurs, 6
Chute, 152
Chef de cuisine, 10
Chemise de nuit, 96
Chemises, 105, 108
Chemisette, 104, 108
Chenil, 62, 63
Chocolates, 29
Choufleur, 21
Cigare, 93
Cigarettes, 92
Cinéma, 63, 128
Cirage, 5
Cirage de chaussures, 5
Cirque, 129
Ciseaux, 49, 95
Citron, 26, 30, 33
Clefs, 2, 52
Clefs (à écrous), 69
Coca-Cola, 33
Cocktail, 32, 33
Coffre à bijoux, 114
Coffre-fort, 2
Coiffure, 38
Collants, 98, 108
Colle, 49
Collier, 110
Collision, 154
Collyre, 86
Cologne, 40
Compartiment pour fumeurs, 58
Concert, 130–31
Concombre, 18
Consigne, 52
Costume de bain, 100
Côte de boeuf, 11
Côtelette d'agneau, 10
Coton, 86
Couchette, 61
Couchettes, 57
Coup de soleil, 154
Coupe de cheveux, 40
Coupure, 152
Courroie, 75
Course à pied, 149
Course d'automobiles, 140
Course de chevaux, 140
Course de taureau, 144
Coussin, 54
Couteau, 9, 47, 151
Couture, 94, 95
Couverture, 5, 64
Crabe, 14
Cravates, 105, 109
Crayon à mine automatique, 46
Crayon pour les sourcils, 88
Crayons, 47
Crème, 5, 30
Crème de beaute, 89
Cric, 68
Cristaux, 117
Croissant, 24
Cruche, 117
Cuiller à soup, 9

Cuillère, 9
Culotte, 97
Culottes de cuir, 119

Danse, 130
Déclencheur, 120
Dé, 94
Dentiste, 158–59
Déodorisant, 87, 88
Dépanneuse, 155
Descente de bain, 3
Desserts, 28–29
Deuxième classe, 59
Diapositives, 123
Diarrhée (remèdes), 91
Dinde, 13
Divertissements, 128–31
Dominos, 132
Douche, 3

Eau, 33, 69
Ebouillantage, 152
Echarde, 152
Echarpe, 101
Echarpes, 116
Eglise, 127
Elastique, 47
Emplâtre pour les cors, 91
Encre, 46
Enveloppes, 5, 46, 48
Epinards, 21
Epingles, 95
Epingles de cheveux, 87
Epingles de cravate, 105
Epingles de sûreté, 89, 91, 95
Essence, 69
Estomac dérangé, 86
Etiquette, 48, 50
Etui à lunettes, 115
Evantail, 113
Examen visuel, 160
Excursion, 124–27
Exposition, 143
Extincteur, 74

Facteur, 45
Fard à paupière, 88
Faux cils, 38
Femme de chambre, 4
Fer à repasser, 5
Fermeture éclair, 104
Feux de circulation, 73
Ficelle, 48
Figurines, 112
Fil, 94, 95
Fil dentaire, 91
Filtre d'air, 75
Flan, 29
Flash, 123
Fléchettes, 132
Football-Association, 148
Fourchette, 9
Fraises, 26
Framboises, 26
Freins, 75
Fromage, 25
Fruits, 26–27
Fume-cigare, 93
Fumoir, 64
Funiculaire, 85

Gaine, 96
Gants, 103, 104
Garage, 2
Gare, 56–59
Gargarisme, 90
Gâteau, 28
Gigot d'agneau, 16
Gilet, 106
Glace, 28
Glace aux fruits recouverte de crème, 28
Glaçons, 4
Golf, 136
Gomme elastique, 47
Gondole, 82
Gonflage, 67
Gravures, 119
Guides, 49
Guitare, 118
Gymnase, 62

Hachette, 191
Haricots de lima, 19
Haricots fève, 19
Haricots verts, 19
Hockey à patin, 141
Homard, 15
Hôpital, 155
Hôtel, 2–5
Houpette, 88
Housse de voyage, 51
Huile de graissage, 69
Huile de table. 31
Huîtres, 15

Imperméable, 102, 107
Infirmière, 155, 159
Insecticide, 90

Jaquette, 106
Jambon, 12
Jarretelles, 104
Jeu de dames, 134
Jeu d'échecs, 133
Jours, 36
Jumelles, 161
Jupe, 98
Jupons, 97, 108

Klaxon, 74
Kleenex, 86

Lait, 33
Lait solaire, 87
Laitue, 18
Lames de razoir, 87
Lampe de poche, 150
Lancer des puids, 149
Lange, 91
Lanterne, 130
Lapin, 13
Laque, 89
Lard, 12
Lavage de voiture, 70
Légumes, 18–21
Lit, 3
Lits jumeaux, 3
Livres, 114
Loupe, 49, 160
Lunettes, 160
Lutte, 146

Macaroni, 22
Malade, 155
Mal à la tête, 86
Mal aux dents, 198
Malle, 53
Manicure, 39, 41
Manteaux, 99
Maroquinerie, 115
Marteau, 69
Mascara, 38
Massage du visage, 40
Médecin, 155, 158–59
Menu, 9
Melons, 27
Mètre à ruban, 95
Métro, 79
Minijupe, 99
Miroir, 77
Mocassins, 106
Mois, 34–35
Monnaie, 6–7
Monter à cheval,
Montre-bracelet, 111
Monuments, 124
Morsure, 153
Morsure d'insecte, 153
Moto, 78
Mouchoir, 105, 116
Musée, 124, 127

Nappe, 118
Natation, 136
Navets, 19
Navire, 60–65
Négatives, 123
Nez, 158
Nouilles, 22

Oeil, 154, 158
Oeuf à la coque, 16
Oeuf dur, 17
Oeuf poché, 17
Oeuf sur le plat, 16
Oeufs, 16–17
Oeufs brouillés, 16
Oignon, 20
Olive, 21
Omelette, 16
Opéra, 128
Orange, 26
Oreille, 158
Oreillers, 5, 64
Os, 159
Ouvre-bouteille, 33

Pain, 24
Pain de seigle, 24
Pain grillé, 31
Palourdes, 15
Pansements adhésifs, 86
Pantalon, 99, 104 108
Pantoufles, 97, 104
Papeterie, 42, 46–49
Papier, 46
Papier à écrire, 5, 46
Papier hygiénique, 3, 90
Paquetage, 151
Parapluies, 102–4
Parasoleil, 121
Par avion, 42

Pardessus, 99
Pare-brise, 77
Pare-chocs, 77
Parfait, 29
Parfum, 110
Passeport, 7
Pastèque, 27
Pastels, 47
Pâte, 22–23
Pâte dentifrice, 87
Patience (jeu de), 134
Patinage, 138
Pêche, 26
Pêcher, 139
Pédicure, 39
Peigne, 87
Peintures, 119
Pellicule, 120
Pendule, 37, 111, 112
Perche, 14
Perles, 114
Permanente, 39
Petit déjeuner, 5
Petit gâteaux, 28
Petit pain mollet, 24
Petit pains, 5, 24
Petit pois, 18
Petit verre à cognac, 33
Petite cuillère, 9
Pharmacie, 86–91
Pied, 159
Pince à cravate, 105
Pince à épiler, 38
Pince-notes, 47
Poivrons, 19
Pipes, 93
Piqûre, 152
Piscine, 63
Piste, 148–49
Planche à repasser, 5
Plume, 46
Pneu crevé, 68
Pneus, 67
Pointe, 116
Poire, 26
Poire à lavement, 86
Poisson, 14–15
Poive, 9
Police, 156, 157
Polo, 145
Pomme, 26
Pommes de terre, 22
Pont, 73
Porc, 12
Porcelaine, 112, 113
Porte-bagages, 50, 51, 55, 74
Porte-clefs, 115
Portefeuille, 115
Portefeuille (perte de), 156
Porte-jarretelles, 96
Porte-manteau, 4
Porte-monnaie, 114
Portier, 4, 50
Posemètre, 123
Poste, 42–45
Poste-radio, 63
Pot d'échappement, 68
Poudre de riz, 88
Poudrier, 88
Poulet, 13
Première classe, 58, 59
Pulvérisateur nasal, 90
Pumpernickel, 24
Punaise, 47
Pyjama, 96, 104

Radiateur, 69
Radiateur électrique, 5
Radio, 118
Radis, 19
Raisins, 26
Rasoir, 87
Rasoir électrique, 87
Restaurant, 8–9, 30–31
Réveil, 5
Riz, 22
Robe, 108
Robe de chambre, 97, 104
Robe de soir, 101
Routes, 72
Robe paysanne, 119
Rodeo, 142
Rosbif, 12
Rouge à joues, 88
Rouges aux lèvres, 88
Roussette, 28
Ruban, 94
Ruban adhésif, 86
Rugby, 145

Sac de couchage, 151
Salade, 31
Salle d'attente, 65
Salon, 55
Salon de beauté, 38–39
Sandales, 108
Sandwich, 31
Saucisse, 11, 12
Saumon, 14
Saut à la perche, 149
Savon, 4, 87
Savon à va sec, 87
Scooter, 77
Sculpture, 112, 114, 119
Se faire attaquer, 156
Sel, 9
Sels pour bains, 88
Semelle orthopédique, 91
Service, 4
Service de table, 113
Serviette, 4, 9, 118
Serviette hygiénique, 89
Shampooing, 38
Ski, 139
Slip, 104, 108
Smoking, 107
Soucoupe, 30
Soupe, 31
Sous-vêtement, 104, 108
Soutiens-gorge, 96
Spaghetti, 23
Sports, 140–49
Station de service, 70
Stewardess, 55, 80
Sucette, 29
Sucre, 5, 9

T-shirt, 108
Tabac, 92–93
Tables, 118
Tablette, 46
Taille-crayon, 47
Talc, 40, 91
Talc "akileine," 86
Tampons, 89
Tarte, 29
Tasse, 30, 58
Taxi, 81
Teinte, 41
Teinture, 39
Telégramme, 44
Teléphone, 4, 63
Télévision, 130
Temps, 34–37
Tennis, 137
Tennis de table, 133
Tente, 150
Thé, 30
Théâtre, 131
Théâtre de marionnettes, 131
Théière, 5, 30
Thermomètre, 90
Timbre-poste, 5, 42, 43
Tire-bouchon, 33
Toilette, 3, 58, 63
Tomate, 18
Train, 56 –59
Traîneau, 84
Transformateur, 4
Transport, 54–59
Trépied, 117, 122
Truit, 14
Tunnel, 71
Tuyau d'échappement, 68

Urgences, 152–57

Vase, 119
Veau, 10
Vélo, 77–78
Ventilateur, 75
Ventilateur electrique, 5
Verre, 33
Vêtement de nuit, 96, 104
Vêtements de plage, 100, 108
Viande, 10–11
Vin, 32
Vinaigre, 31
Visite médicale, 158
Voiture, 66–75
Voiture de louage, 87
Vol, 54
Volaille, 13
Volant, 75
Volant au filet, 132
Voleur, 156–57
Voltage, 4

Wagon-restaurant, 57

Yeux, 160

ITALIANO

Accappatoii da bagno, 97, 104
Accendi-sigari, 93, 115
Accetto, 191
Acconciatura, 38
Aceto, 31
Acqua, 33, 69
Aeroporto, 54
Affrancatura, 43
Agi, 94
Agitazione di stomaco, 86
Aglio, 20
Agnello, 10
Albergo, 2–5
Albicocca, 29
Alpinismo, 135
Ambulanza, 155
Ananasso, 27
Anello, 110–11
Anguria, 27
Anitra, 13
Antiacido, 86
Antistamini, 90
Appunta lapis, 47
Aragosta, 15
Arancia, 26
Arganetto idraulico, 68
Argenteria, 112
Aria, 67
Articoli di cucina, 116
Ascensore, 2
Asciugamano, 4
Asicella, 152
Asparagi, 18
Aspirina, 86
Assalto corporale, 156
Assegno di viaggio, 6
Astuccio, 88
Astuccio dei gioielli, 114
Attaccapanni, 4
Autobus, 80–81
Automobile, 66–75
Autorimessa, 2
Autostrada, 71

Bagaglio, 50–53
Bagno, 3
Balletto, 129
Ballo, 130
Banana, 27
Banca, 6
Bar, 64
Barbabietole, 19
Barca a remi, 83
Baseball, 146
Bastoncello di sapone per la barba, 87
Batteria, 75
Baule, 53
Benda, 154
Benzina, 69
Berretto, 107
Bibite, 32–33
Biblioteca, 65
Bicchiere, 33
Bicchiere d'acquavite, 33
Bicicletta, 77–78
Bigliardo, 137
Biglietti, 56
Binocolo, 161
Binocolo da teatro, 161
Birra, 32
Bistecca, 11
Blusa, 98, 109
Bocchino, 93
Bocchino per cigari, 93
Bombe, 28
Borotalco, 40
Borsa dell' acqua calda, 86
Borsa, 114
Borsa (la perduta de la), 156
Bottiglia per bambino, 91
Bottoncini, 105
Bottoni, 94–95
Bowling, 135
Braccialetto, 111
Brettelle, 104
Brocca, 117
Broccoli, 20
Bruciatore di sole, 154
Bruciatura, 152
Burro, 25
Buste, 5, 46, 48
Busto, 96

Cabina, 61
Cablogramma, 45, 63
Caccia, 138
Caduta, 152
Caffè, 30
Caffettiera, 5, 30
Calcio, 148
Calzamaglia, 98, 108

Calze, 97
Calzini, 105, 108
Calzoni, 99, 104, 108
Camera di scrivera, 65
Camera telegrafica, 63
Cameriera, 4, 55, 80
Camicetta, 98, 109
Camicia da notte, 96
Camicie, 105, 108
Camicie da notte, 96, 104
Camiciola, 104, 108
Campeggio, 150–51
Candelabro, 113
Candele, 150
Candele d'accensione, 75
Canile, 62–63
Canottiera, 108
Canotto, 83
Cappello da spiaggia, 108
Capello di pioggia, 102
Capo cuoco, 10
Cappelli, 100–101, 107
Cappotti, 99
Caramella con lo stecchino, 29
Caramelle, 29
Carciofo, 20
Carne, 10–11
Carne di maiale, 12
Carota, 18
Carozza, 81
Carozza ristorante, 57
Carta, 46
Carta da lettere, 5, 42, 46
Carta igienica, 3, 90
Carta stradale, 49
Cartiera, 46–49
Cartoline, 132
Casinò, 130
Cassaforte, 2
Cassetta postale, 44
Catene per gomme, 68
Cavatappi, 33
Caviglia slogata, 153
Cavolfiore, 21
Cerotto, 86
Cerotto per i calli, 91
Cetriolo, 18
Chiave inglese, 69
Chiavi, 2, 52
Chiesa, 127
Chitarra, 118
Chiusura lampo, 104
Ciglie finte, 38
Ciliegie, 26
Cinema, 63, 128
Cinghia, 51
Cintura, 104, 109
Cintura igienica, 89
Cinture di salvataggio, 74
Cioccolate, 29
Cipolla, 20
Cipria, 88
Cipria per bambini, 91
Circo, 129
Clacson, 74
Clistere, 86
Coca-Cola, 33
Cocktail, 32–33
Colla, 49
Collana, 110
Colonia, 40
Coltello, 9, 47, 151
Concerto, 130–31
Coniglio, 13
Coperta, 5, 64
Corda, 51
Corrida de toros, 144
Corse, 149
Corse ippiche, 140
Corso automobolistica, 140
Coscia d'agnello, 10
Costate di manzo, 11
Costolette d'agnelo, 10
Costumi da bagno, 100
Cotone, 86
Cravatte, 105, 109
Crema, 5, 29, 30
Crema facciale, 89
Crema per la barba, 87
Cristalleria, 117
Croissant, 24
Crostatina, 29

Cucchiaino, 9
Cucchiaio, 9
Cucire, 94–95
Cuenta, 31
Cuffia da bagno, 91
Cuoiame, 115
Cuscino per sdraio, 54

Dama, 134
Denaro, 6–7
Dentista, 158–59
Deodorante, 87–88
Diapositive, 123
Diario, 49
Diarrea, (rimedie), 91
Doccia, 3
Dolci, 28–29
Dolor di denti, 198
Domino, 132
Doni, 110–19
Disco sul ghiacchio, 141
Ditale, 94
Divertimenti, 128–31

Elastici, 47
Elmetto, 77
Emergenze, 152–57
Esamenazione oculare, 160
Estintore, 74

Facchino, 50
Fagioli, 19
Fagioli di lima, 19
Fagiolini, 19
Farmacia, 86–91
Fazzoletto, 105, 116
Fazzoletti di carta, 86
Ferita, 152
Ferma cravatta, 105
Ferro da scaldare elettrico, 5
Ferro da stiro, 5
Fettuccini, 22
Fiammiferi, 9, 93, 160
Filo, 94–95
Filo dentario, 91
Filtro d'aria, 75
Forbici, 49, 95
Forcelle, 87
Forchetta, 9
Formaggio, 25
Frac, 101
Fragole, 26
Francobolli, 5, 42, 43
Freni, 75
Frutta, 26–27
Fungi, 20
Funicula, 85

Gabinetto, 3, 58, 63
Galleria, 71
Gambero, 14
Ganci, 95
Gargarismi, 90
Gelato, 28
Gelato misto, 28
Giacca, 106
Giarrettiera, 96
Gioielli, 110
Giorni, 36
Giuco dei dardi, 132
Giuoco dei pezzi, irregolari, 134
Giuoco del calcio, 145
Gocce per occhi, 86
Golf, 136
Gomma da cancellare, 47
Gomma forate, 68
Gomma sgonfiata, 68
Gomme, 67
Gondola, 82
Gonna, 98
Granchio, 14
Granita, 29
Guanciali, 5, 64
Guanti, 103–4
Guardaroba, 52
Guide, 49

Impermeabile, 102, 107
Inchiostro, 46
Incisione fotografiche, 119
Indumenti da spiaggia, 100, 108
Infermiera, 155, 159
Insalata, 31
Insetticida, 90
Investimento, 154

Ladro, 156–57
Lamette, 87

Lampa tascabile, 150
Lampadina, 4
Lampo al magnesio, 123
Lamponi, 26
Lancio, 149
Lanterna, 130
Lapis per sopracciglio, 88
Latte, 33
Lattuga, 18
Lavaggio di macchine, 70
Lederhosen, 119
Legumi, 18–21
Lente d'ingrandimento, 49, 160
Letto, 3
Letto matrimoniale, 3
Letti gemelli, 3
Libri, 114
Limone, 26, 30, 33
Lista, 9
Lotta Romana, 146
Lozione per abbronzare, 87
Lucido, 5
Lustrascarpe, 5

Macaroni, 22
Macchina, 66–75
Macchina cinematografa, 122
Macchine fotografice, 120–23, 157
Maglíe, 102, 104 105, 108
Maglione, 98
Maiale, 12
Mal di testa, 86
Manicure, 39, 41
Manzo, 11
Martello, 69
Massaggio, 40
Matita a sfera, 46
Matita per le labbra, 88
Matite, 47
Matite di cera, 47
Medico, 155, 158–59
Mela, 26
Melanzana, 20
Meloni, 27
Mesi, 34–35
Messa in piega, 38
Metro automatico, 95
Minigonna, 99
Moccasini, 106
Moletta, 47
Monumenti, 124
Morso d'animale, 153
Mostra equina, 143
Motocicletta, 76
Motopattino, 77
Motoscafo, 83
Museo, 124, 127
Mutande, 104
Mutandine, 97, 104, 108

Naso, 158
Nastro, 94
Nastro per cucire, 94
Navi, 60–65
Negativi, 123
Nuotare, 136

Occhi, 160
Occhiali, 160
Occhio, 154, 158
Olio per condire, 31
Olio per motore, 69
Oliva, 21
Ombrello, 102–4
Ombretto per occhi, 88
Omeletta, 16
Opera, 128
Orecchini, 110
Orecchio, 158
Orologio, 37, 111–12
Orologio da polso, 111
Ospedale, 155
Ossi, 159
Ostrica, 15

Palestra, 62
Pallacanestro, 147
Panciotto, 106
Panciotto a maglia, 98
Pane, 24
Pane di segala, 24
Pane tostado, 31
Panecetta, 12
Panini, 5, 24
Panino imbottito, 31
Pannilino, 91
Pannilino igienico, 89

Pantaloni, 99, 104, 108
Pantofole, 97, 104
Parabrezza, 77
Paracolpi, 69
Passaporto, 7
Pasta, 22–23
Pasta dentifricia, 87
Paste, 28
Patate, 22
Pattinare sul ghiaccio, 138
Paziente, 155
Pedicure, 39
Pellicola, 120
Penna, 46
Pennello da barba, 87
Pepe, 9, 19
Perle, 114
Permanente, 39
Pesca, 26, 139
Pesce-persico, 14
Pettine, 87
Piaga, 152
Piattino, 30
Piatto, 30
Piccola slitta, 84
Piede, 159
Pigiama, 96, 104
Pinture, 119
Pinzette, 38
Pipe, 93
Piscina, 63
Piselli, 18
Pista, 148–49
Poliziotto, 156–57
Pollame, 13
Pollo, 13
Polo, 145
Polsini, 105, 111
Polvere per i piedi, 86
Pomodoro, 18
Ponte, 73
Popone, 27
Porcellana, 112, 113
Portabagaglio, 55, 74
Portabaglio, 88
Portacenere, 118
Portachiave, 115
Portafogli, 115
Portaocchiali, 115
Portavivande, 117
Posta, 42–45
Posta aerea, 42
Posti per dormire, 57
Posti per sedere, 55
Postino, 45
Prima classe, 59
Prima colazione, 5
Profumo, 110
Proscuitto cotto, 12
Pugilato, 144
Pumino per la cipria, 88
Pumpernickel, 24
Puntina, 47
Punture d'insetto, 153

Quaderno, 49

Radiatore, 69
Radice, 19
Radio, 118
Ragazzo d'albergo, 4
Rapa, 19
Rasoio, 87
Reggipetto, 96
Rimmel, 38
Riso, 22
Ristorante, 8–9, 30–31
Rodeo, 142
Rosaio elletrico, 87
Rosbif, 12
Rossetto, 88

Saco a pelo, 151
Sala da fumo, 64
Sala da riposo, 55
Sale, 9
Sali da bagno, 88
Salmone, 14
Salone di barbiere, 40–41
Salone di bellezza, 38–39
Salsiccia, 11–12
Sandali, 108
Sapone, 4, 87
Scacchi, 133
Scarpe, 98, 106, 108
Scarpe da tennis, 108
Sciampagna, 32
Sciare, 139
Sciarpe, 116
Scompartimento per fumare, 58
Scotch tape, 47
Scottatura, 152

Scultura, 112, 114, 119
Seconda classe, 59
Sedano, 18
Sedia, 112
Sedia a sdraio, 64
Semafori, 73
Servizio, 4
Shampoo, 38
Sigarette, 92
Sigaro, 93
Silenziatore, 68
Smoking, 107
Soprabiti, 99
Sotterranea, 79
Sottoveste, 97, 108
Spaghetti, 23
Spagho, 48
Spazzola, 40
Spazzola per i capelli, 87
Spazzola per scarpe, 5
Spazzolino da denti, 87
Specchio, 77
Spilli, 95
Spilli di sicurezza, 89, 91, 95
Spinaci, 21
Sport, 140–49
Spruzzatore nasale, 90
Spruzzatore per i capelli, 89
Statuette, 112
Stazione di servizio, 70
Stazione ferroviaria, 56–59
Stivali, 99, 102, 106, 109
Stola, 101
Strade, 72
Stufa elletrica, 5
Sveglia, 5

Tabacco, 92–93
Tacchino, 13
Taglierini, 22
Taglio di capelli, 40
Tampone d'orecchio, 90
Tamponi, 89
Tappetto da bagno, 3
Targhette, 48, 50
Tartina per tè, 24
Tassi, 81
Tavola da stiro, 5
Tavole, 118
Tazza, 30, 58
Tè, 30
Teatro, 131
Teatro delle marionette, 131
Teiera, 5, 30
Tela gommata, 86
Telefono, 4, 63
Telegramma, 44
Televisione, 130
Tempo, 34–37
Tenda, 150
Tennis, 137
Tennis da tavola, 133
Termometro, 90
Termos, 151
Tingere i capelli, 39
Tinta per i capelli, 41
Torta, 28
Tovaglia, 118
Tovagliolo, 9, 118
Transformatore, 4
Transporto, 54–59
Treno, 56–59
Treppiede, 122
Trota, 14
Tubetti di ghiacchio, 4
Tubo di scappamento, 68

Uova, 16–17
Uova strapazzate, 16
Uovo bollito, 16
Uovo fritto, 16
Uovo in camicia, 17
Uovo sodo, 17
Uva, 26

Vagone letto, 61
Valigia, 51
Vaso, 119
Ventaglio, 113
Ventaglio cinturino, 75
Ventilatore, 75
Ventilatore elettrico, 5
Vestiti, 99, 106, 108, 109
Vino, 32

Visita medica, 158
Visita-turistica, 124–27
Vitello, 10
Volante, 75
Voleggio, 149
Volo, 54
Voltaggio, 4
Vongole, 15
Zaino, 151
Zeppole, 28
Zucchero, 5, 9
Zuppa, 31